Gayle Soucek

Gouldian Finches

Everything About Purchase,
Housing. Nut~~~~~ ~~~~~~ ~~~~~~~
and Breedin~

BARRON'S

2 CONTENTS

INTRODUCTION TO THE GOULDIAN FINCH

Northern Australia is a beautiful yet harsh environment. Summer monsoon rains turn quiet streams into raging rivers, and the stifling heat and humidity never dissipates. Marshes and lakes form, and then recede as the rains fade. In the dry winter season, the arid heat causes trees to drop their leaves and undergrowth to die back, leaving endless open savannas of tough grasses edged with scrubby forests. Wildfires rage across the land, scorching everything in their path. It is in this punishing environment that one of the most beautiful birds in the world makes its home.

Natural History

The Gouldian finch, *Erythrura gouldiae* (formerly C*hloebia gouldiae*), acquired its name from the famous ornithologist John Gould, who named the breathtaking finch in honor of his wife Elizabeth. Because of this, it is often referred to as the Lady Gouldian finch. Historically, these birds ranged across most of Northern Australia, from the western Kimberley region to the Cape York Peninsula of Queens-

Gouldians are sometimes referred to as Painted finches or Rainbow finches.

land in the East. They were once considered common, but populations have declined rapidly due to disease and habitat damage. Gouldians are now considered endangered, with only an estimated 2,500 mature birds left in the wild. Small fragmented populations exist throughout Western Australia and the Northern Territory, but they are uncommon in Queensland.

Reasons for Decline

The Australian government has instituted a recovery plan, but the reasons for their decline are varied and complicated. In the wild, Goul-

Other Names

Due to its brightly colored feathers, the Gouldian is sometimes referred to as the Rainbow finch or the Painted finch. Other common names are the Lady Gouldian finch, or simply "Goulds."

dians prefer to nest in tree cavities (especially *Eucalyptus* trees) that are within a short distance of watering holes.

Diet: Their diet consists of various grass seeds and insects. During the dry season, they survive on sorghum and spear grasses. In the wet season, they shift to cockatoo grass, golden beard grass, and various types of spinifex grasses. They relish a variety of insects, even raiding spiders' webs for their bounty. In fact, some experts believe that Gouldians become almost entirely insectivorous during breeding season.

Grazing: Unfortunately, their intimate yet tenuous relationship to the land leaves the Gouldian finch especially vulnerable to habitat and climactic changes. Much of the land is now used as grazing areas for cattle, buffalo, and horses. In some areas, feral pigs trample or uproot the grasses. Grazing prevents grasses from going to seed, so pastoral areas provide precious little food to sustain finch populations.

Wildfires: In addition to livestock damage, seed production is greatly impacted by the voracious wildfires that rage across the grasslands during the dry season. In the time before European settlers came to the area, the native Aboriginal people intentionally burned small patches of land each season to create natural firebreaks in the landscape. Today, wildfires burn uncontrollably, sometimes traveling vast distances. As the impact of humans on the landscape and the climate becomes more obvious, wild populations of finches and other seed-eating birds continue to decline.

Parasites: Humans, however, aren't the only problems facing wild Gouldians. In the 1980s, researchers discovered a high incidence of air sac mites (*Sternostoma tracheacolum*) in wild finches. Parasites such as these, along with other disease agents, present a dire threat, especially against already stressed populations.

Solutions

With all these factors converging upon them, it's easy to see why Gouldian finches are suffering declines in the wild, but perhaps that trend will ultimately reverse. Currently, several agencies, including the Australian government and the World Wildlife Fund are working in concert on a national recovery plan for the Gouldian finch. Their plans encompass land management, habitat restoration, reintroduction, and disease control. A large part of the effort also includes community participation and education, so that people will understand and work to save this endangered Australian treasure.

The Gouldian in Captivity

The outlook for captive Gouldian finches is much rosier. Once considered extremely fragile and difficult to breed, domestically bred birds are proving to be hardier than their wild counterparts. They're still not considered a good choice for beginning aviculturists, but as we gain a greater understanding of their needs and preferences, they are beginning to thrive in captivity. Indeed, captive populations greatly exceed the number of wild birds, which will be a boon to reintroduction efforts.

Captive breeding began in the late 1800s about the time when Gouldians were first imported into Europe. The earliest documented captive breeding occurred in 1888 in the aviaries of the Australian Museum in Sydney, but shortly after that, English aviculturist Reginald Phillips successfully bred several different color varieties of Gouldians. In the years between 1930 and 1946 another English aviculturist, P. W. Teague, bred a bloodline spanning 24 generations. Mr. Teague meticulously documented his work in British avicultural magazines, providing priceless guidance to other fanciers.

In 1960 the Australian government banned exports of its native birds, leaving the birds already in captivity to serve as founder stock for future generations. Thankfully, many devoted aviculturists swapped knowledge and bloodlines to create a healthy and diverse captive population that continues to flourish, and might someday serve as a genetic reservoir to enhance wild populations through reintroduction programs.

Physical Description

The Gouldian finch is a sturdy little bird, approximately 5 to 5$\frac{1}{2}$ inches (127 to 140 mm) in length, and weighing about $\frac{1}{2}$ ounce (15 to 20 g.) The males are slightly larger than the hens, and have a longer tail. The two middle

Throughout the book, we will refer to various parts of the Gouldian's anatomy: (1) crown, (2) nares, (3) upper mandible, (4) lower mandible, (5) throat, (6) breast, (7) front toes, (8) hind toe, (9) hock, (10) cloaca (vent), (11) tail, (12) upper tail coverts, (13) rump, (14) wing, (15) back, (16) nape.

The red-headed color morph is the dominant or "normal" coloration.

Gouldians can be found in a wide variety of color mutations.

tail feathers are long and sharply pointed, giving the bird quite an aerodynamic appearance. The beak is conical and mostly horn colored, with a reddish tip. The legs and feet are pink and well scaled, and the eyes are brown.

Color Morphs

In the wild, there are three naturally occurring color phases in Gouldian finches: black-headed, red-headed, and yellow-headed. The black-headed is the most common color morph in the wild, accounting for approximately 75 percent of wild birds. The red-headed color morph is dominant to the black-headed gene, even though they are outnumbered about three to one by black-heads in the wild. The reason for this involves the manner in which the black-headed gene is passed to offspring, and we'll discuss that in a later chapter. The yellow-headed form (in which the head is actually orange or red-orange) is very rare in the wild, but is less scarce in captivity.

Red-headed Color Morph

As mentioned, the red-headed is the dominant, or "normal" coloration. Male birds have a deep red face mask outlined in black feathers that cover the chin area and give the bird a bearded appearance. Behind the black feathers is a halo of beautiful turquoise blue feathers that merge into a grass green coloration of the neck, back, and wings. The rump and upper tail covert feathers are sky blue, silhouetted against black tail and primary wing feathers. The breast is deep purple or bluish purple above an orange-yellow abdomen, which fades into white around the legs and under the tail. The undersides of the wings are a silvery gray.

Females are similar in coloration, but the colors are noticeably duller and less pronounced. The turquoise neck feathers are either absent in the hens or greatly reduced, and the bird might have a somewhat "washed-out" appearance. Juvenile birds are mostly dull shades of green and gray, giving little hint to the rainbow of colors they'll sport after their first molt.

Black-headed Color Morph

The coloration of the black-headed Gouldian is almost identical to that of the red-headed Gouldian, with the exception of the face mask. As the name states, these birds have a black mask. If they inherited the black gene from both parents, they will have a solid black mask and red-tipped beak. If there are tiny red or yellow feathers mixed into the black mask, or if the beak is yellow-tipped, it indicates that the bird has red- or yellow-headed genes in its genetic makeup. As mentioned earlier, because the visual characteristic of the black mask can be passed down through many different genetic combinations, it is the most common color variety, even though it is not a dominant genetic trait.

Yellow-headed Color Morph

The yellow-headed morph is extremely rare in the wild, but is being bred more regularly in captivity. The term "yellow-headed" is actually quite misleading, because these birds display a mask that is usually a rusty red-orange, although various shades of orange and yellow exist. In hens, it can display as a brownish orange peppered with black feathers. The remainder of their coloration is very similar to the red- and black-headed types.

The yellow-headed trait occurs when a gene mutation creates an inability to properly synthesize carotenoids into red pigments. This gene mutation in a genetically red-headed bird causes the mask coloring to appear orange as the red is suppressed. To phrase it another way, any bird that displays visually as yellow-headed is actually a red-headed displaying this genetic trait. A black-headed bird that is affected by the yellow mutation will look almost identical to a normal black-headed, except that the tip of the beak will appear yellow instead of red. The lack of red pigment is visible in the beak, but is hidden by the pigments in the black feathers. In this case, the bird is carrying two genes for the yellow mutation even though it displays a black head.

Other Color Varieties

The three color types described above are the only naturally occurring variations, but selective breeding of captive birds has led to several color mutations that affect breast color, back color, or overall color. Following is a brief description of the most common Gouldian finch mutations:

✔ White-breasted: The white-breasted mutation was first produced in Australian aviaries in the early 1950s. It can occur in any of the three color morphs, and the resulting birds have a pure white chest instead of the normal purple chest.

✔ Lilac-breasted: The lilac-breasted mutation appeared in the 1970s, and displays as lilac or rose-colored feathers in place of the normal purple. Typically the hens display a lighter lavender color.

✔ Blue-breasted: This difficult-to-breed mutation appeared in the mid 1970s, but is not easily maintained in bloodlines. It displays as medium blue feather color on the chest, which tends toward a lighter blue in hens.

✔ Blue-backed: The blue-backed mutation eliminates yellow pigments in the birds, causing normally green feathers to appear as blue, and normally yellow feathers to appear as cream-colored or off-white. This mutation first appeared in Australia in the 1960s.

✔ Yellow-backed: This mutation, also known as lutino, suppresses blue and black coloration, resulting in birds that are primarily yellow. Depending on the other genes present, the mask color can vary from red to gray. The melanistic eye color is absent, so these birds appear to have red eyes instead of the normal brown.

✔ Dilutes: Dilute mutations occur when a male bird inherits only one gene of the yellow-backed mutation. This suppresses some of the black and blue coloration of his feathers, so the bird will appear "washed out" or diluted in color. Because of the sex-linked characteristics of this trait, hens cannot display the dilute trait.

✔ Silvers: The silver mutation was first bred in the Netherlands, and it occurs when a bird inherits both the yellow-backed and blue-backed genes. In this case, all the colors are muted to such a degree that the resulting bird is a rather plain pale grayish cream color. Silvers can occur in either sex.

✔ Albino: True albinos lack all pigment, including eye pigmentation, so they appear as pure white with red eyes. Some all-white birds with dark eyes are occasionally bred, especially in the Netherlands, but these are not pure albinos; usually these birds are the result of breeding lutino (yellow-backed) birds with pastel color varieties. On close inspection, these dark-eyed birds will usually display hints of cream or yellow feathers, especially on their chest or face mask area. True albinos tend to be very fragile and short-lived.

Differences in color can be subtle or dramatic, depending on a bird's gender, genetic makeup, or overall health.

Gouldian Finch Behavior

Gouldian finches are generally steady and easygoing birds. They are not noisy, communicating mostly through a series of soft chirps or trilling songs. Their voices are pleasant, so they are good choices even for apartment dwellers. They are active and curious, and will spend a great deal of time moving about the cage. In captivity, they have been known to live past ten years of age, but six to eight years is a more common life span. In the wild, their life is much shorter, perhaps only about three years. With good care, your Gouldian will bring you pleasure for many years!

How Many Birds?

Gouldians are very social birds, so they should never be kept as a single pet. Unlike parrots, they don't form pair bonds with humans; because of this, a single Gouldian caged alone will be lonely and miserable. If you intend to breed them, then the logical choice is to acquire a suitable pair and set them up in a breeding cage. If you want to keep them as pets, same-sex pairs—either two males or two females—should coexist happily and enjoy each other's company, especially if they're placed together when they're both young. It's never a good idea, however, to mix an unequal number of Gouldians when both sexes are present, or the birds will form pairs and then terrorize the remaining single bird. If you have multiple finches in a cage, and you see one being chased or harassed by the others, you must immediately remove it from the cage and house it separately, or it won't survive.

Mixed Aviaries

Mixed aviaries are another option if you have enough space to devote to a large flight cage.

Provided there is sufficient room, Gouldians will live happily with other species of similar-sized, seed-eating finches, including zebra, society, Bicheno's (owl) finches, and canaries. Never house finches with hook bill birds such as budgies or other small parrots, however, because parrot-type birds are more aggressive and have much greater beak strength. Even if the small parrots don't attack or threaten your Gouldians, the finches will likely become ill just from the stress of being caged with potentially dangerous housemates. As mentioned earlier, if you ever see any bird that is being picked on, chased, or kept away from food dishes by the others, remove it to safety.

Other Pets

Most household pets are a threat to your finches, so keep your birds securely caged and away from danger. Dogs, cats, ferrets, and snakes are all predators, and will see your Gouldian as nothing more than a flying snack. Even very tame and gentle dogs will have a hard time understanding that the brightly feathered flying thing isn't a toy to be pounced on and retrieved. It's true that dogs sometimes befriend parrots, which are typically larger and are not as fluttery. Parrots also have very strong and sharp beaks, which helps to remind other pets to proceed with caution. Your finch is defenseless, however, and it will depend on your common sense to keep it from harm. Always keep your finches caged, and place the cage in a location safely away from curious noses and paws.

Children

Because of their small size, and peaceful and gentle manner, Gouldians are safe pets to have around children of any age. However, finches do not like to be handled, and the loud shrill voices and rapid movements of young children might frighten them. If you do have young children in the home, they should be taught to approach the birds slowly and to use their "inside voices" when around the cage. Your birds will quickly get used to normal household noise levels, but don't set up the cage in a place where kids play and roughhouse on a regular basis. On the other hand, don't stash the birds in a remote room of the house where they have little interaction with the family, or they might become bored and depressed. Usually, a protected spot in a corner of a family room is a great location. From that vantage point, your Goulds will be able to observe and interact with people, yet they will still feel safe and won't have to contend with kids and dogs bumping into their cage at every turn.

Elderly or Handicapped Family Members

Gouldians can make wonderful companions for those who are housebound. Their soft chirps and songs are enchanting, but are not loud enough to disturb even the most sensitive individuals. Gouldians aren't prone to many zoonotic (transmissible to human) diseases, although if someone in your household is immuno-suppressed, then be sure to have any new pets checked carefully before adding them to your home. Mixed aviaries of finches and canaries have become very popular in many nursing homes because the cheerful little birds are masters at brightening the day of any observers. Recent studies have proven that pet ownership lowers blood pressure, reduces depression, and might lessen loneliness. The companionship that pets provide, and the care that they require, can even reduce symptoms of dementia in the elderly. Learning to care for pets is also a wonderful way for children to learn compassion and responsibility.

With all that pets give to us, they require comparatively little in return: proper food, water, housing, and a little love. Please keep in mind that although Gouldians are relatively low maintenance, they are most definitely not maintenance-free! If you choose to share your life with these birds, remember that these are endangered and precious creatures, not throw-away short-term amusements. If you make the commitment to provide the care they need, they will reward you with their beauty and charm for many years to come.

BUYING A GOULDIAN FINCH

A healthy Gouldian Finch is a beautiful sight to behold, dancing effortlessly through its environment like a rainbow in motion. It is bright-eyed, alert, and joyously interactive. It's nearly impossible to watch one of these colorful characters without finding a smile crossing your face.

An unhealthy bird, however, is quite a different animal. Huddled on the perch glassy-eyed and weak, a sick finch is a sad sight indeed. Gouldians have had a long reputation as fragile and difficult-to-keep birds, but this is mostly undeserved. In their native environment, they thrive amid some of the harshest conditions on earth. Unfortunately, they were first brought into captivity en masse, with little understanding of their dietary or environmental needs. Early captive birds succumbed to disease and malnutrition at an alarming rate. They were soon known as a species for experienced bird keepers only.

As our knowledge of aviculture grew, so grew the pool of healthy breeding stock.

Healthy birds from a quality bloodline will bring you years of pleasure and companionship.

Today's domestically bred Gouldians are reasonably hardy birds that can live a long and healthy life in captivity as long as they're provided with good food, clean and spacious caging, and necessary medical care. Of course, you must start with a healthy bird in the first place. Please do not buy a bird that is in poor condition in the hopes that you can rescue it. Although this is an understandable reaction for a compassionate person, it is a heartbreak waiting to happen that can cost you dearly in money, time, and emotional investment. If you have other birds at home, you also will be putting their health at risk. If you see a sick bird for sale, notify the seller and move on.

Where to Find a Bird

The first step in buying a healthy bird is finding a reputable seller. Gouldians are becoming

CHECKLIST

Choosing a Healthy Bird

✔ Begin by observing the bird from a distance: Is it active and alert, or lethargic and depressed? Healthy birds are busy moving about the cage, vocalizing, eating, or preening. Sick birds often sit hunched in a corner.

✔ When you move close to the cage, how does it react? Healthy, well-socialized birds will view you with interest, and might even come closer and chirp to you. Sick birds will either move away or stay put, but they will likely look weak or withdrawn. Poorly socialized birds might thrash wildly trying to escape, and will probably avoid eye contact.

✔ How do the bird's eyes look? Healthy birds have bright, clear eyes with no sign of any discharge or swelling. Sick birds might have eyes that are partially closed, swollen, or showing signs of discharge. The eyes probably look dull or even cloudy.

✔ How is it holding its feathers? A healthy and wide-awake bird appears sleek and its feathers are held tight against its body. A bird with fluffed-out feathers is either sick, cold, or sleepy. A sleepy or cold bird will usually snap to attention and tighten its feathers as soon as a person approaches. If it continues to stand with fluffed feathers while you are near, it is most likely ill.

✔ Is there any nasal discharge? Does the bird appear to be panting or short of breath? Is it breathing with its mouth open? Does its tail bob up and down with each breath? These are all warning signs of respiratory distress and disease.

✔ Are its feathers bright and clean, or do they look dusty or raggedy? Poor feathering is a sign of sickness, malnutrition, parasites, or abuse by cage mates. Soiled feathers around the head can indicate respiratory or gastrointestinal disease infection.

✔ Does the bird move around the cage easily, or does it appear lame or unsteady? These can be a sign of injury or severe illness.

✔ Is the bird thin? The best way to check weight in a finch is to examine the keel bone (breastbone) that runs down the center of the chest. A bird in normal weight will have a keel bone that is barely visible, with good fleshing on either side. A sick bird will have a prominent, almost sharp keel bone, and its chest will appear sunken. Thin birds are either sick or malnourished.

✔ How do its droppings look? Healthy birds have droppings that are well formed, and consist of dark green feces, white urates, and clear urine. If the droppings are runny, yellowed, or tinged with blood, the bird is ill. Certain food items can temporarily change the appearance of droppings, but don't take the chance.

✔ How old is the finch? Youngsters are easy to spot, because they don't yet have their adult plumage. Some signs of old birds are poor feathering, very rough scaling on feet and legs, and stiffness of movement due to arthritis. Try to purchase a Gouldian that is about six months old. They're old enough to be strong and hardy, but young enough to provide you with years of companionship.

increasingly popular and more widely available, but they are by no means common. If you are seeking a specific genetic profile for breeding purposes, you might have to do some sleuthing to track down the bird you're after. If you're just looking for a Gouldian or two as pets your search should be much simpler. Unless you live in a remote area, it's likely that you can find a source near your home. Let's discuss a few possibilities.

Pet Stores

Pet stores are an obvious option for many reasons: they're usually abundant in populous areas, they're accessible, and you can return to them if you have a problem. They might not carry a large variety of birds (unless that is their specialty) but most stores carry at least a few finches, so it is possible they'll have Gouldians. If they don't have any Gouldians in stock, they might be willing to acquire some for you. If not, the people who work at the shop can still be a valuable resource to aid you in choosing supplies and food, and they might be able to direct you to local finch breeders or avian veterinarians.

Before you make any purchases, spend some time looking around and asking questions. Here are a few thoughts to consider:
✔ Is the store clean?
✔ Are the birds kept in clean and appropriate conditions?
✔ Is there plenty of food and fresh clean water available in each cage?
✔ Are cages overcrowded?
✔ Do the birds have appropriate perches, swings, and toys? (Gouldians do not typically play with toys, but they will relish a swing.)
✔ Are they fed any fresh foods? The best stores usually offer some chopped fruits or veggies to their birds.

TIP

Plan Ahead

Before you bring your bird home, have a suitable cage set up and all necessary supplies ready. If you purchase a cage at the same time you buy the bird, it will have to remain in the travel box while you set everything up. This is unnecessarily stressful for your finch! Please plan ahead and have everything ready in advance for its homecoming.

✔ Is the store well stocked so that you can rely on it for your food and supplies?
✔ Does the store offer a health guarantee on the birds?
✔ How knowledgeable are store personnel?

A sick bird will have difficulty perching, and will usually sit with fluffed feathers and partially closed eyes.

If you are comfortable after the above considerations, then you've probably found a good source for your bird and its supplies. If you don't have ready access to a quality pet shop, or if your local store does not sell Gouldians, then there are several other options.

Bird Fairs

In many communities, one of the surest signs of spring is the proliferation of bird fairs hosted by area bird clubs. These one-day fairs usually bring together breeders and suppliers from a wide area. It can be a great opportunity to meet local finch breeders, ask questions, purchase supplies, and look at birds for sale. If you

Don't buy any bird on impulse, even though you might find yourself enthralled by the Gouldian's beauty.

go this route, however, you must proceed with great caution. Although probably most of the vendors are hard working and honest aviculturists, I have seen too many cases of dishonest frauds who use bird fairs as dumping grounds for sick or compromised birds. Don't be afraid to ask for references and check them carefully. Often the vendors are either members of the hosting club or are locally known, so checking references might be as easy as walking down the aisle a few booths and speaking with other bird folks. When shopping at a bird fair, many of the considerations listed previously for pet stores apply. Due to space limitations, the birds might be in temporary travel cages that seem a little small, but they should still be clean, filled with fresh food and water, and be protected from drafts, other birds, and the poking fingers of curious fair-goers.

If you do find a bird you like, please do not buy on impulse. Be certain you have an appropriate cage and other supplies already set up at home. Do not buy a bird unless you are prepared to bring it straight home and place it in its new accommodations. Walking around a hot, crowded fair building with your new Gouldian stuffed into a paper bag or cardboard carrier is a sure way to stress and sicken the bird. Make sure you have all the necessary contact information from the seller so that you can reach him or her if you have any questions later about the bird or its health or diet.

Finally, keep in mind that a Gouldian purchased from a bird fair has a higher likelihood of disease exposure than one purchased from a

Look for stores that keep their birds in clean and uncrowded conditions.

breeder's home. Birds at a fair are stressed, frequently crowded, and are sitting in a confined area near hundreds of other birds of many species. That's not to say that you can't find a healthy and wonderful bird at one of these events, but always proceed with caution and common sense. If you have unfortunate dealings with anyone at a club-sponsored event, always notify the club (there is usually a contact name on flyers advertising the event). Although they probably won't be able to help solve your problem, they at least can take steps to insure that the disreputable vendor is not allowed to sell at any future fairs.

Gouldian Breeders

Buying direct from a reputable Gouldian breeder is one of the best ways to find a good

Keep any new birds caged separately from existing birds in your home until a suitable quarantine period has passed.

selection of healthy birds. Breeders range in size and experience from hobbyists who have a single pair of birds in their living room to commercial operations that have hundreds or even thousands of birds. In aviculture, the size of the operation has nothing to do with quality—experience with Gouldians, and a sincere fondness for the birds are what count.

Before you speak with or visit a breeder, draw up a list of questions and concerns you might have. Most fanciers are enraptured with their chosen species, and will gladly share knowledge and advice. Don't, however, expect them to offer tours of their breeding facilities. Strangers in an aviary present many risks, including disease transmission, breeding disruption, and security issues. If they feel comfortable offering a tour, great, but never expect or demand one.

If you intend to breed your Gouldian at some point, then you should ask the breeder about your bird's parentage. Without a clear understanding of its genetic makeup, you won't know how to choose an appropriate mate for it, and you'll have difficulty determining what colors of chicks to expect. Good record keeping is one of the hallmarks of a high-quality breeding program, so it's essential to start off on the right foot.

Banding: Most (but not all) bird breeders will band their birds to make record keeping easier. What this means is that the aviculturist slips a solid metal or plastic ring over the chick's foot and onto its ankle when it is still very young. As the chick grows and its feet become larger, the band cannot be removed unless it is cut off. This method serves as an indication that the bird was bred in captivity, because a closed band can't be forced onto the ankle of an adult bird without either injuring the bird's foot, or

using a band that is much too loose and large.

Most closed bands are engraved with the breeder's initials or aviary identifier, the state, if in the United States, a numerical code that identifies that particular bird, and the year the bird was hatched and banded. Banding is not required by law in any of the states (at least not yet), so the bands are sold commercially or provided by various avicultural organizations. As such, the information included can vary depending on the source or breeder's preferences, and bands are not usually traceable. Some organizations provide traceable bands and keep a registry, but many do not. Bands are still a valuable tool to use as identifiers within an aviary, however, or to prove ownership of lost or stolen birds.

To find a Gouldian breeder in your area, check with local avian veterinarians or bird clubs. You can also check state listings of breeders in magazines such as *Bird Talk* or *Birds USA*.

The Internet

The realm of cyberspace has opened astonishing new doors for trading products and services, and that includes selling Gouldian finches! It's now possible to sit in the comfort of your living room and purchase a bird half a continent away. Although the Internet can seduce us with endless choices and possibilities, it has also opened up a Pandora's box of problems inherent to long-distance commerce.

When you buy a bird on the Internet, you are essentially buying blindly. Despite what the seller tells you, you're not there to observe the bird, to hold it in your hand and feel its weight, or to study its demeanor for signs of illness. Once you send off your money, you have precious little recourse if the bird never arrives at your door. Yes, fraudulent sales are against the law, but most police departments are busy enough with local crime and community issues, and won't have the manpower or resources to investigate Internet fraud. Sometimes other agencies might get involved, but they usually confine their efforts to large-scale fraud cases, and won't be inclined to exert a lot of effort on a bird sale transaction that is just a few hundred dollars. Sad to say, but small-time Internet scammers often operate with virtual impunity from the law.

There are, of course, hundreds of ethical and devoted breeders who sell their birds via the Internet. The trick is to make sure you know whom you're dealing with. Following are a few hints:

✔ Ask for professional references. Customer references are easy to fake, but references from a veterinarian, pet shop, bird club, or from other well-known aviculturists are likely to be genuine. These pros will not risk their hard-earned reputation by vouching for an unethical thief.

✔ Study their web site carefully. It's true that any grade-schooler with a computer can slap together a web site, but a true finch fancier will likely have a site filled with pictures and information about their birds. This is of course no guarantee of honesty, but lack of a professional appearance can be a red flag.

✔ Trust your instincts! A reputable breeder will be concerned about finding a proper home for his or her birds, and will be very cautious about shipping during weather that is exceptionally hot or cold. A scam artist will be concerned only about how fast you can send the money. If you sense any pressure to "close the sale," proceed with caution.

✔ Ask intelligent questions. An experienced Gouldian breeder should be glad to offer any advice you need to keep the birds happy and healthy. If the person seems to lack knowledge, or answers you in an evasive or impatient manner, think twice about buying from that person. Of course, you should always respect the breeder's time, and don't pepper him with basic questions that you should have known the answers to before you moved to this point in your search.

✔ Get it in writing! This applies to health guarantees, shipping arrangements, and any other parts of your transaction that could come back to haunt you at a later date. For example, if you agree to buy a one-year-old bird, and it shows up on your doorstep with a band that indicates it is five years old, you will have no recourse unless you have something in writing that proves the seller has violated your agreement.

✔ When possible, contact breeders through bird community web sites that work to eliminate fraudulent posts and expose scammers. Two excellent sites are *www.upatsix.com* and *birdsnways.com*.

Despite the above warnings, buyers aren't the only ones who are at risk on the Internet. Crooks use breeder postings to target them for theft, and sellers can also be vulnerable to fraudulent certified check schemes. The Internet is a wonderful tool, but like any tool, it must be used with caution.

Shipping Birds

If you buy your bird locally, you need only a small travel cage or sturdy cardboard box to transport it safely home in your car. If you are buying from a distant breeder, however, it's a

Some sellers will have Gouldians in a variety of ages and colors. Look for a young bird in the color of your choice.

lot more complicated and expensive. The only safe way to ship birds long distances is by air. Companies that ship by ground are not usually able to accommodate live animals, and will not accept them as cargo. Unfortunately, shipping by air is neither cheap nor easy.

Since the terrorist attacks of 9/11, most airlines will accept cargo only from "known shippers." What exactly this means varies by airline, but suffice it to say that not just anyone can bring in a package for shipment by air. In addition, many airlines do not accept live birds for shipping, probably due to the perception that they are fragile and difficult to transport. There are a few airlines, however, that gladly ship birds, and they usually do a very good job of it. I have purchased birds from around the country on many occasions, and I have never had any problems.

Once, a bird I purchased was on a flight through a connecting city, and the connecting flight was canceled due to major snowstorms. The airline personnel retrieved my bird from the grounded plane, brought it into their offices, and kept it warm and occupied until another flight became available. They called to let me know of the delay, and stayed in frequent contact as the evening wore on. Even though hundreds of human travelers were stranded overnight by the storms and forced to sleep in airport waiting areas, my new bird got VIP treatment and was hustled onto the only other flight that made it out that night. He arrived in perfect condition, no worse for the wear.

Use a sturdy box or transport cage to bring your new birds home.

Cost

Shipping by air is not cheap—expect to pay between $125 and $200 for the airfare, depending on the airline. The shipper is also required to provide a health certificate signed by a veterinarian before the airlines can accept any live animal. Some sellers absorb this cost, but if they don't, it will add about $15–$50 to the cost of shipping. In addition, the bird must be contained in an airline-approved carrier, which will likely add about $25 or more. If you add it all up, a $100 finch can easily end up costing double or triple that amount when it is shipped by air.

Experienced and caring keepers will provide you with a Gouldian that is healthy and beautiful. Avoid "bargain" birds.

Aside from the obvious financial implications, shipping can be stressful to birds. If at all possible, try to find a Gouldian locally. If you cannot, and you decide to have a bird shipped to you, follow some simple rules:

1. Get a precise itinerary, including flight numbers and any stopover information before the bird ships. Ask the seller to book a direct flight whenever possible so you don't run the risk of canceled connecting flights.

2. Ask the seller to provide food and water in the bird's carrier. That way, if the flight is delayed, your new pet will not suffer from dehydration or hunger. If the Gouldian knows how to drink from a bird water bottle, one of those should be fastened in the carrier. If not, then a shallow dish with a soaked sponge inside will provide a thirsty finch some water without danger of it all spilling out in transit. Be sure to find out exactly what the breeder has been feeding so that you can offer familiar foods when you get the bird home.

3. Before you head to the airport, arm yourself with a list of phone numbers. Make sure you have contact information for the breeder who sold you the bird, the person who actually handed the bird over at the airport (if it was not actually the breeder), and numbers for the cargo and customer service contacts at the airline. You will also need to show identification before you're allowed to pick up any shipment, so come prepared.

4. If the flight is delayed, contact an airline representative immediately for an update. Typical short delays due to air traffic or minor weather aberrations are just an inconvenience, but a major delay or a missed connecting flight could endanger your finch. If such a problem occurs, speak to an agent and explain that there is an exotic bird on the flight, and ask the agent to help. After all, the airline is responsible for the bird's welfare, and will usually do whatever it can to ensure it arrives safely at its destination.

Home at Last

If you've followed my advice, you already have a suitable cage set up and ready for the new arrival. If you don't have any other birds, then you don't need to worry about quarantine. Simply place the Gouldian into its new cage, offer it plenty of food and fresh water, and leave it alone so that it has time to check out its new surroundings. Resist the urge to hover over the bird, and keep kids and other pets at a distance.

Do your best to acclimatize it slowly if it has shipped from a radically different climate. For example, if your new Gouldian was being kept outdoors in Arizona during the summer, and you are acquiring it during a Minnesota winter, the bird should be kept in an extra warm room—(75–80°F [24–27°C])—until it settles in and adapts to its new home. Captive-raised Gouldians are not as fragile as the original imported birds, and will soon adapt to normal household temperatures, but a little extra warmth during transitional times and stressful periods helps them to cope.

Quarantine

If you do own other birds, then it's important for their health, as well as the health of your new Gouldian, to follow quarantine procedures. True quarantine is a complicated process that takes into consideration such things as airflow patterns and strict sanitation measures, and it's pretty difficult to achieve in a typical household. You should aim for a method of quarantine that, at the very least, keeps new birds in a separate room and prevents people and pets from tracking germs from one room to the next.

Because certain diseases have very long incubation periods, or can exist in asymptomatic carrier birds, quarantine is never a guarantee that diseases can't spread. A 60-day quarantine will, however, allow you to identify any obviously sick finches and get them treatment before they infect others. It also gives new birds a chance to settle in and get used to their surroundings without the added stress of coping with a new and unfamiliar flock.

Creating Quarantine

To create quarantine, place the new arrivals in a separate room, preferably on another floor in your home. If you have forced-air heating, close the vents in the quarantine room to prevent any diseases from being carried throughout the house. If closing the vents isn't possible, you might be able to tape a furnace filter over them. This won't be effective for blocking all pathogens, but it will help. Get in the habit of feeding and cleaning your existing birds first, and then service the newcomers. Always wash up (shower and change clothes if possible) before you handle your old birds. The same goes for other family members and pets too—no walking back and forth between old and new birds—or they can spread any diseases that might be present.

Cleaning Tools

When you're cleaning cages or bird rooms, always use separate cleaning utensils. If you use the same microbe-laden sponge and broom in and out of quarantine areas, you're defeating the whole process. If you must use certain objects in both places, spray or wipe them with a disinfectant or bleach solution (one ounce bleach per one quart water) and let them dry thoroughly before use. To kill most microorganisms, disinfectants need at least ten minutes of contact time to be effective, so don't just spray on and immediately wipe off. Also keep in mind that fumes from bleach and other disinfectants can be highly toxic to birds, so always use them in a well-ventilated area. Sometimes a good dose of fresh air is wonderful for dispersing germs and toxins, so open a window if the weather permits! Air cleaners and purifiers also serve to capture any airborne pathogens, and I recommend their use in any area where birds are kept.

Warmth and Humidity

While your Gouldians are in quarantine, keep their area warm and well humidified. You don't need to treat them like hothouse flowers, but a little extra warmth will help them to deal with the stress of a new home. Normal home temperatures are fine, but just make sure you protect them from drafts in the winter and air conditioner vents in summer. If you're living in a cold northern climate, humidifiers are a great way to keep Gouldians comfortable during excessively dry indoor winter humidity. Keep in mind that these birds come from a very hot and humid climate, so they'll appreciate a little extra moisture during the winter.

After about 60 days (or as your veterinarian advises) you can move the new finches into the same area as your other birds. By this time, they have likely heard each other, and they're no longer total strangers. However, it's still important to wash your hands between handling different birds, and keep the cages clean to prevent germs from gaining a foothold.

HOUSING YOUR GOULDIANS

Your Gouldian's cage is its home: the place where it sleeps, eats, perhaps raises a family, and feels safe from the dangers of the world. It must be sturdy, comfortable, and large enough to keep your finch happy. You are the housekeeper who must clean and service this home, so you'll be happiest if the cage is of quality construction, is easy to clean, and lends quick access to perches, trays, and food dishes.

The Cage

A good cage will make both of you happy. You'll want to spend almost as much time choosing a cage as you do choosing your finch. If you buy a cage that is unwieldy and hard to clean, you might begin to resent the time spent caring for your bird, or worse, you might unwittingly risk your Gouldian's health by doing a substandard job of cleaning.

Cage Styles

There are a variety of cages in every shape, style, and material on the market today. Some are well made and highly functional, while others are flimsy and poorly designed. Others are strictly intended for decorative purposes,

A well-equipped cage will help keep your birds healthy and happy.

and aren't designed to hold a live bird at all. The following hints can help you choose.

✔ Always purchase a cage from pet or aviary suppliers. If you find a cage at a department or home goods store, it is most likely designed as a decorative item, and probably contains paint or other material that would be toxic to your finch. It is, of course, safe to buy from *pet departments* in department stores, but they probably won't have a large selection available.

✔ Think simplicity. Ornate cages might be beautiful, but they are usually more difficult to keep clean. Oddly shaped cages, such as round cages or those with pagoda-style roof compartments can frustrate or confuse your finch. Unfortunately, many cage companies design such impractical styles because they're aesthetically pleasing to humans. The best shape is a rectangle that is both tall and long. Finches like to fly, so a long cage is important, but they'll enjoy some height too. Very tall, narrow cages aren't pleasing to your finch, because finches can't really fly very well vertically.

✔ Choose a high-quality metal or Plexiglas cage design. Wooden or bamboo cages are impossible to clean and disinfect properly, and won't last long. Wire cages with plastic bases and trays are okay, but the plastic tends to warp, stick, and crack over time. You'll save money and aggravation in the long run by spending a little more for a cage with a metal base and tray. Another option is Plexiglas or glass aviary-type cages. These are usually built into an attractive wooden cabinet, giving them the look of a nice piece of furniture. These can be pricey, but they allow you a clear view of your birds, and they do a good job of keeping the mess contained. Plexiglas is easy to clean and disinfect, but it can become hazy or cloudy over time if it's not maintained with very gentle cleansing methods. Glass cages will withstand tough scrubbing, but of course are more fragile than Plexiglas.

✔ Look carefully at the access doors and feeding doors. You'll want a door that is large enough to allow you to service the cage easily, but not so large that your finch zips past you and out of the cage every time you open it. Some manufacturers make cages that have a "door within a door." These styles have a large access door for cleaning and rearranging the cage when the bird is not in it, and also incorporate a smaller door that is just large enough to allow a human to reach inside without allowing the bird to escape. Make sure that all doors operate easily but close securely. If possible, choose a cage style that provides for at least three dishes: one for water, one for seed,

and one for fresh foods. I recommend that you buy an extra set of dishes so that you always have clean dishes available.

✔ Check the bar spacing. The bars must be placed so that your Gouldian cannot push its head between the bars and become trapped. Usually $1/2$-inch (12.7 mm) spacing is suitable for finches. Make sure there are no gaps or openings in the cage that can trap a curious bird.

✔ Buy the largest cage possible. Your Goulds likely will spend the rest of their lives in this cage, so give them plenty of room to exercise. The minimum cage size for a pair of Gouldians is approximately 14 inches wide by 16 inches tall by 30 inches ($35 \times 40 \times 76$ cm) long. Keep in mind that this is a minimum size. A larger cage, especially one that is longer, would be preferable. If you're keeping more than two birds, the cage will need to be proportionately larger to accommodate all the occupants without fighting and overcrowding.

✔ You will also need a sturdy stand or cabinet on which to place the cage. Be wary of flimsy stands that can easily be knocked over by kids or pets. Also, if you choose a cabinet stand, you'll be able to stash supplies and food safely out of sight.

✔ Avoid buying a used cage. Used cages might harbor parasites and pathogens that can be difficult to eradicate. The finish will likely be worn or even rusty, making cleaning a nightmare. Also, you might not be able to purchase replacement parts. In my experience, used cages are rarely a bargain.

Cage Accessories

Once you have a suitable cage, your next step is to furnish it. You'll need at least a variety of perches and cups, and perhaps a swing and cage cover. The cage you purchased probably came with some perches and cups, but these likely won't be sufficient. As mentioned earlier, you'll need at least three cups in the cage, and a duplicate (or even triplicate) set will make your life easier. When you service the cage in the morning, you can toss the dirty dishes in the dishwasher and still have a fresh set ready to go. That way your birds always have sparkling fresh cups available. Look for cups made of heavy-duty plastic, stainless steel, or ceramic. Galvanized metal cups can leach toxic metals, and are difficult to clean thoroughly. Cheap plastic cups are safe, but they'll dry out, stain, and crack easily, so you'll be replacing them often.

Perches

Think of perches as footwear for your finches. You wouldn't want to wear the same pair of shoes every day of your life, and neither will your birds. A bird that is forced to stand all day on a uniform diameter perch is likely to develop foot or hock sores from the constant and unchanging pressure points. You'll need to provide a variety of perch textures and diameters to help your birds exercise their feet. Look for perches that are $1/4$ inch to $1/2$ inch (12.7 mm) in diameter. Natural branches make wonderful perches, and can often be found in pet shops. You can also use branches from your backyard trees, but if you do so you must disinfect them thoroughly. I usually wash them in hot soapy water, rinse well, and dry them in my oven at 200°F (93°C) for about an hour. That will kill most pathogens and protect your finches from diseases carried by outdoor birds.

Materials: Perches are also available in a wide variety of other materials, including cement, plas-

TIP

Perch Placement

Arrange perches so that your finch has room to fly in the cage. Birds usually prefer to sleep at the highest point in the cage, so place a sleeping perch near the top. Place other perches to provide easy access to food and water, but always avoid positioning any directly above the dishes, or the Gouldians will likely perch above and foul the food or water with droppings.

tic, and rope. Cement-type perches, also known as pedicure perches, can provide your Gouldian with a non-slip surface that will help to wear down its nails. Many birds also use these to wipe their beaks, thereby removing flaky patches. Some pedicure perches are made of minerals, and are actually edible. Others are formed from terracotta or sand. In any case, your Gould will likely enjoy having one of these in its cage.

Rope perches are flexible and soft, and are easy on tender feet. They're difficult to clean properly, however, and they become a danger when frayed—a bird can get its toes tangled in the fibers and break a leg. If you choose a rope perch, replace it when it gets dirty or worn. You can clean rope perches by running them through your dishwasher and then drying thoroughly, but this doesn't always do a good job of removing all the stains. Once again, make certain that they are completely dry before you put them back in the cage, or the damp material will make a great breeding ground for bacteria and fungi.

Arrange perches so that your birds have plenty of room to flap their wings and move about.

Other Accessories

Gouldians don't play with toys, but they usually delight in a swing. I suggest you get one wide enough to accommodate at least two birds at a time to prevent quibbling over who gets to use it. I'd also recommend a millet spray holder. Millet sprays are a favorite Gouldian treat, and there are several types of holders on the market that will make it easy for you to hang a spray in the cage.

Another accessory to consider is a cage cover. Birds need plenty of sleep—at least ten hours a night—so you might want to get in the habit of putting your Goulds to bed early so that they're not tempted to stay up and watch television with the rest of the family. A cage cover provides darkness and a sense of security for the

Suitable finch cages are widely available at pet shops and on the Internet.

Braided-rope perches are popular and comfortable for birds, but replace them if they become frayed or worn. Your finch could become entangled in loose fibers and break a leg.

birds. Of course, you can use a large towel or any other piece of dark fabric, but make sure that your finches can't get tangled in loose threads or heavy looped nap.

Lighting

If your Gouldians are housed indoors, then it's critical to provide the proper lighting to keep them healthy. Birds (and people) depend on ultraviolet rays from the sun for a variety of metabolic processes, especially vitamin D production. Indoor birds will not have access to sunlight, so you'll need to provide a substitute. Please don't think that simply placing the cage

near a window will do the trick. Window glass (and plastic) blocks about 99 percent of the beneficial ultraviolet rays. Your birds might enjoy the view and the warmth from sunlight streaming in a window, but it won't provide them with the light waves they need to synthesize vitamins.

The best way to provide artificial sunlight is to use full-spectrum lighting near the cage. There are several wonderful brands of full-spectrum bulbs on the market, including Ott-Lites, Vita-Lites, Verilux, and Chromalux. Most of these companies sell both bulbs and a variety of fixtures so that you can choose the style that works best for you. These lights closely

═══ TIP ═══

Shade

Never place a birdcage directly in front of a window that receives full sunlight, or the birds can overheat. Make sure that at least a portion of the cage is shaded so that the finches can move to a cooler spot if they choose.

mimic natural sunlight, and will help to keep your birds healthy and happy.

One word of caution: Don't use bulbs that are marketed strictly for reptiles. Most of these are designed to enhance a reptile's color, and don't always provide the balanced spectrum of light that birds require.

Air Quality

Fresh air is something we tend to take for granted, but indoor birds are exposed to fumes from household chemicals, cooking odors, dust, and a host of bacteria and fungi that float through the air and congregate in enclosed spaces. You, in turn, will be exposed to feather dander and aerosolized feces from your finches, which can aggravate allergies and asthma. To keep everyone healthy, consider adding an air purifier to your home.

Air purifiers draw air through various filters that remove pollutants and odors. Look for HEPA purifiers, which will remove most contaminants. HEPA is an acronym for "High Efficiency Particulate Air" filtration. These filters were developed during World War II by the Atomic Energy Commission to remove radioactive particles from the air, so they'll most likely do a good job of removing dried bird poop! Air purifiers are typically rated by how many cubic feet of air they can process in a minute, or CFM. The higher the CFM, the more powerful the purifier. Be certain to purchase one that is large enough to purify the area you plan to place it in, and keep the filters clean as recommended by the manufacturer.

Cleaning the Cage

Once your birds are settled, you'll need to set up a regular schedule for cleaning and maintenance. What you do, and how often you do it, will depend a great deal on the number of birds you own. For example, a single pair of Gouldians in a relatively compact cage will require a lot less upkeep than a floor to ceiling mixed aviary that is filled with dozens of finches. Following are some guidelines:

Daily:

1. Wash and replace all food and water dishes. Use hot soapy water, or run them through the dishwasher to sanitize them.

2. Change cage paper or substrate daily. I recommend using plain or waxed paper or newsprint for cage bottoms. Substrates such as sand, pine shavings, corncob, or ground walnut shells look nice, but they provide a breeding ground for mold, bacteria, and parasites. They can also be quite messy if your birds flap their wings and toss the litter around. To make daily paper changes a breeze, place a week's stack of papers on the cage floor and just remove the soiled top sheet each day. Paper also makes it much easier to keep an eye on your bird's droppings for any early signs of illness. Cage litter tends to absorb or disperse droppings so that it's nearly impossible to see what they look like.

3. Scrape any accumulated droppings off perches. Most pet supply houses sell wire perch scrapers, or use a sturdy bristled brush.

4. Sweep up any debris around the cage. An accumulation of tossed seeds and molted feathers can attract insects and mice, so take a minute to keep the area clean.

Weekly:

1. Remove the cage tray and scrub it thoroughly in hot soapy water. Be sure to dry it carefully before replacing to prevent rusting. I use my hair blow dryer to dry the trays in a flash.

2. Use a soft damp cloth to wipe down the cage bars. If water alone isn't enough, there are several enzyme-based products on the market that are designed to safely dissolve bird droppings. One popular and nontoxic product is named "Poop-Off," and it is widely distributed through pet supply outlets. Don't ever use chemical cleaners on the cage while your Goulds are in it, unless they are specifically intended for use around birds.

3. Remove and scrub fouled perches as necessary. Discard and replace any perches that are damaged or impossible to clean.

As Needed:

1. Periodically, you should remove your birds from the cage to give it an "overhaul." Place them in a temporary or travel cage, and be sure to provide a supply of food and water. Remove all cage accessories, perches, trays, and dishes. Depending on the size of the cage, either place it in a sink or bathtub, or drag it outside. Scrub the entire cage with hot soapy water. Be sure to get into all the cracks and crevices where

CHECKLIST

Cleaning Supplies

✔ Soft clean cloths for wiping down cages. Cloth diapers or microfiber cloths are excellent at cleaning, and won't scratch surfaces.

✔ A spray bottle filled with water. You can add a little vinegar to cut dirt more effectively.

✔ A wire brush and scraper for cleaning perches.

✔ A medium-bristled brush (plastic or natural) to scrub trays and other surfaces.

✔ Baking powder. It's a wonderful and safe mild abrasive for scrubbing stubborn spots.

✔ Enzyme cleaners such as Poop-Off for removing dried droppings.

✔ Broom, whisk broom, and dustpan.

✔ Paper towels for drying or quick cleanups.

✔ Gentle nontoxic soap for scrubbing cage items in hot water. Dish soaps work well for this purpose.

✔ Disinfectants. Some popular brands are Nolvasan, Wavicide, Oxyfresh, Roccal, and Pet Focus. Disinfectants are typically divided into low-level, intermediate, and high-level classifications. Low-level disinfectants will kill most bacteria and fungi, and some viruses. Intermediate-level disinfectants will kill almost all bacteria and fungi, and many viruses. High-level disinfectants kill all pathogens. Ask your veterinarian for recommendations to choose the best one for your purposes. Keep in mind that disinfectants are strong chemicals, and careless use can be more dangerous than not using them at all.

Outdoor cages require special attention to prevent insects, rodents, and wild birds from spreading disease.

Clean cages and perches can help prevent pathogens from making your finches ill.

parasites can hide. Rinse thoroughly, then spray down the cage with disinfectant. Allow the disinfectant to work for the recommended contact time (see manufacturer's directions), then rinse again. Allow the cage to dry thoroughly before returning the birds.

2. Replace perches, cups, and any accessories that are worn or stained. Check the cage for signs of rust, bent or broken bars, or any sharp edges that could injure your finches.

3. For breeding pairs, remove and replace nest boxes. Wooden boxes can't be effectively disinfected, so they must be replaced at minimum once a year, preferably after each clutch.

How often you perform the "as needed" steps will depend on many factors. You should *always* disinfect the cage after a disease outbreak or parasite invasion. If your birds are healthy and you're not experiencing any problems, however, perhaps a once a year "spring cleaning" is all that's required. It's important to use common sense when doing a major cleaning. Of course you want to keep your Gouldians clean and healthy, but capturing them and removing them from the cage to disinfect it is stressful to the birds. A certain low level of pathogens in the environment is normal, so don't feel that you must keep the cage as sterile as a hospital operating room. Your good judgment and your bird's apparent health will be your best guide.

Clean or replace nest boxes at least once a year, preferably after each clutch.

If you live in a warm climate, you might wish to keep your birds housed outdoors. Even in colder climates, Gouldians will do fine if kept outdoors just during the warm summer months.

Where to Build the Aviary

Your first step is to determine the proper site. It should be close to your home, both to deter thieves, and to allow you to keep an eye on the birds and service them easily. It should allow full sunlight to reach part of the aviary, but should include a partially shaded area so that the birds can escape the midday sun if they choose.

Note: Before you begin construction, be sure to check zoning laws in your area. Some towns prohibit outdoor animal enclosures or limit how and where they can be built. A few phone calls up front might save you a lot of aggravation down the road.

Building Materials

Base: Next, you must build a base and a frame. The ideal base is a concrete pad, but if that's not feasible you can use patio blocks. I don't recommend using sand, gravel, or dirt as a floor, because these are impossible to keep clean, and they make good hiding places for parasites. Some aviculturists choose to use dirt planted with various grasses to give the Goulds a more natural setting. This is attractive, but it will greatly increase your birds' exposure to parasites, especially worms that need to spend part of their life cycle in the dirt. Concrete and patio blocks certainly aren't a guar-

antee that your aviary will remain parasite-free, but at least you can do a more thorough job of cleaning.

Frame: For framing, use either wood two-by-fours or cinder blocks to create upright pillars. Wood is, of course, much easier to work with, but it can rot and might need to be replaced after several years. Cinder blocks create a more permanent structure, but one that can't be relocated if you change your mind on placement. If you use cinder blocks, you'll still need wood to frame off the roof and doors. Decide which will best fit your needs and your construction skills.

Sides and roof: After the frame is built, cover the sides and roof with hardware cloth or galvanized wire mesh. Be sure the wire spacing is small enough that your finches can't wriggle through and escape! You should bury the wire at least 12 inches (30 cm) into the ground on all sides to prevent predators such as raccoons and foxes from digging their way in and feasting on your finches. I also suggest covering the entire roof (or at least a substantial portion of it) with a solid covering, such as sheet fiberglass. This will serve two purposes: it will

An outdoor aviary can be built against a garage or porch for additional shelter and security.

OUTDOOR AVIARY

shelter your birds from the weather, and it will prevent outside birds and animals from pooping into the cage and spreading disease.

Opossums, for example, are frequent carriers of *Sarcocystis falcatula,* a parasite that can cause severe disease or death in your flock. If an opossum climbs onto the open roof of the enclosure and urinates or defecates, your birds can be infected. They'll still get plenty of sun and some rain through the sides of their flight, but they'll be much more protected with a roof. Of course, none of these measures are foolproof in terms of protecting your birds from disease, so watch closely for signs of illness or parasitic infections.

Doors

Obviously, you'll need a door to access the aviary for cleaning and maintenance. Make sure that the door is framed tightly, and that there are no gaps that can allow a bird to escape. I recommend securing it with a padlock to deter thieves or curious children who might otherwise simply walk in. A single-entry door, however, presents another problem: how to prevent the finches from escaping when you enter. Gouldians are fast and expert flyers, and will easily rocket past you to freedom as you open the door.

Double doors: The best way to prevent this is to build your aviary with a double-door entrance. What this means is that you should add a small, enclosed vestibule with its own door that you enter before entering the aviary. You will close the vestibule door behind you *before* you open the aviary door. That way, if a finch does fly out, it will simply be trapped in the vestibule and can easily be shooed back into the flight cage.

Mosquito netting: If a double-entry door sounds like too much construction, there is another solution, albeit not as safe or effective.

Sturdy mesh cages are suitable for outdoor use, provided they are properly sheltered.

You can use mosquito netting to loosely tent the entire aviary. When you enter, slip under the netting and make sure it reaches down to the ground behind you before opening the door. If any of the birds fly out, they'll be trapped in the netting. Please don't assume that you can do without these safety precautions by simply "being careful." I guarantee that one or more of your Gouldians will eventually escape when you enter, and an escaped Gouldian will not survive very long on its own.

Shelters

Always provide your finches with a shelter if you're keeping them outdoors. It can be as elaborate as an attached garden shed, or as simple as large wooden nest-type boxes hung along the top of the aviary. Whatever you choose, the birds must have some place to escape and stay warm in foul weather. Either have appropriate indoor cages that you can temporarily relocate them to in such emergencies, or devise a method of providing auxiliary heat to the shelters. Some breeders use oil-filled radiator-style space heaters to provide safe radiant heat, but these require electricity to run them, as well as protection from the elements.

HEALTHY NUTRITION

Food is so much more than just sustenance! An ideal diet will keep your bird healthy, help it to reach its maximum life expectancy, and provide it with pleasure and even entertainment during the course of each day. To deny your Gouldian the joy of a diverse and enriching diet is to deny it one of the basic necessities of life.

A bird might survive for quite a while on a poor diet, but it will never thrive. Malnutrition causes or exacerbates a wide variety of disease processes and almost always results in premature death. Because diet is so important, you'll want to spend some time planning how to feed your new pet. The food must not only be healthy and enticing for your Gouldian, but it must also be easy for you to acquire, store, and prepare, or feeding time can turn into an unpleasant chore.

The Basics

To begin with, it helps to have a basic understanding of what constitutes a healthy diet. All

The proper diet will keep your Gouldian vibrant, beautiful, and healthy for years to come.

creatures require a balanced mix of protein, fat, and carbohydrates to provide energy, act as the building blocks for growth, and provide necessary vitamins and minerals. An overabundance of these elements causes obesity and metabolic problems, but a lack leads to malnutrition, stunted growth, and even death. The quality of these elements is important too—incomplete proteins, refined carbohydrates, and an excess of saturated fats can supply too many calories but not enough vitamins and minerals, resulting in a bird (or animal or human) that is obese yet malnourished.

Water

In addition, all creatures require water to sustain life. Water cools the body, removes waste products, and transports nutrients to the cells. Although your Gouldian can derive some water from its food, it's not enough to keep it

TIP

Clean and Fresh Water

Keep clean and fresh water available to your bird at all times! Bacteria and mold grow quickly in standing water, so wash and refill the water dish at least once a day, preferably twice. If you wouldn't want to drink old, stale water, don't expect your bird to drink it.

alive. Without a constant source of fresh, clean water, your finch would die within days, perhaps within 24 hours. Many birds have died an unnecessary death because their keepers inadvertently forgot to replace the water dishes after cleaning.

If all this sounds complicated, don't be concerned. It's really pretty simple to create a

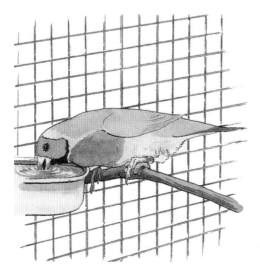

healthy diet for your pet, provided you offer a variety of fresh and nutritious foods. Let's take a brief look at where these elements come from, and how they fit into your bird's diet.

Protein

Proteins are known as the building blocks of life because they are found throughout almost every part of the body. Muscle, flesh, skin, beaks, bone, blood, and feathers are all comprised of protein, and depend on a constant supply of dietary protein to rebuild and repair. Protein can be either animal or vegetable in origin, but all proteins are made up of substances called amino acids. There are approximately 22 amino acids that have been identified, and how they are combined determines the type of protein. The body can manufacture some amino acids, but others can be obtained only from food. Those that must come from food are referred to as "essential amino acids."

Animal foods, including meat, milk, and eggs, contain all the essential aminos and are considered a complete protein source. Plant-based foods, such as grains, seeds, nuts, and legumes (beans), contain some of the essentials, but not all. In order to obtain a complete protein from vegetable sources, it is necessary to eat them in various combinations. We do that almost every day in our lives, although we usually don't give it much thought. Every time you eat a peanut butter sandwich you are combining legumes (peanuts) with grain (bread) to form a complete protein. Bean and rice dishes are another popular form of protein combining. That's why it is

Always keep fresh water available to your finches. A small bird without water can dehydrate and die in less than one day.

important to offer your Gouldian a variety of foods to make sure that its protein needs are being met. You can offer your pet animal protein in the form of insect food or hard-boiled eggs, you can offer a variety of vegetable proteins, or ideally, you can provide an array of both.

Carbohydrates

Carbohydrates are derived mainly from plants, and they act as fuel for the body. They are composed of starches, sugar, and fiber, and provide energy and support for metabolic processes. When carbohydrates enter the body, they are quickly converted into glucose, a simple sugar that travels through the bloodstream and fuels the cells. If too much glucose is present, the excess moves into the liver, where it is converted into glycogen and stored in the muscles and the liver for a backup source of energy. Once the muscles and liver are fully stocked, the liver then turns any remaining glycogen into fat for long-term storage. It's a simple process, and one that is painfully familiar to anyone who has watched a slice of pie or bag of potato chips take up residence on his or her hips.

Unfortunately, the same process affects your Gouldian. Although carbohydrates are essential for health, too much of a good thing can cause obesity, especially in pet birds that are likely more sedentary than their wild cousins. To make matters worse, much of the food we eat is made with highly processed and refined carbohydrates. These are foods that have been stripped of their fiber and most of their essential nutrients. Refined carbs, such as white rice and white flour, are basically empty calories and have no place in your bird's diet. When feeding carbohydrate-rich food, always aim for natural and minimally processed foods.

Fats

In our weight-obsessed culture, dietary fats have gotten an undeservedly bad reputation. Although too much fat is harmful, fat plays a critical role in the body. Fats aid in the absorption of some vitamins, act as precursors for certain hormone-like substances, serve as a reserve source of energy, and provide insulation for the body. Rather than avoid all fats, it is much more important to consider the type of fat in the diet. Fats, also referred to as *lipids*, are divided into three basic categories: saturated, monounsaturated, and polyunsaturated. The length of the molecules contained in the fatty acids that comprise the fat, along with the amount of hydrogen they contain, determine whether a fat is considered saturated or unsaturated. Highly saturated fat contains the most hydrogen atoms, whereas unsaturated contains the least. Almost all fat sources have a combination of these acid molecules, but they are ranked according to their predominant type.

Saturated fats: Saturated fat is derived mostly from animal products, although coconut and palm oil are also highly saturated. Saturated fat is solid at room temperature, and this is the type of fat that is implicated in heart disease and other inflammatory and degenerative diseases. Foods containing saturated fat should be avoided, or at least fed in very limited quantities.

Unsaturated fats: Unsaturated fats come primarily from plants and fish. Unsaturated fats are liquid at room temperature, and depending on their structure, they are known as *monounsaturated* or *polyunsaturated*. These are the healthy fats that should make up part of your Gouldian's balanced diet. Monounsaturated fats are especially healthy, and are found in olives, canola (rapeseed), and peanuts. Corn, sesame,

Captive birds cannot forage like their wild counterparts, so they are dependent on you to provide a nutritious diet.

and safflower are primarily polyunsaturated. These too are healthy, although a high ratio of polyunsaturated to monounsaturated oils has been linked to various inflammatory problems.

Trans-fat: Another type of fat that has been in the news recently is trans-fat. This is a man-made fat that is created by injecting extra hydrogen atoms into unsaturated fats. This process, known as *hydrogenation*, creates an inexpensive fat that is solid and relatively stable at room temperature, which makes it exceptionally popular for bakery and junk food items. Most stick margarines and vegetable shorten-

ings are hydrogenated. Research has proven that trans-fat is extremely unhealthy, so much so that new legislation requires it to be listed on nutrition labels. Some cities are going so far as to ban it from use in restaurants. It goes without saying that this type of fat has no place in your bird's diet, so please don't offer junk food to your pet!

Vitamins

Vitamins are organic substances that regulate cellular functions. A bird that is deficient in one or more vitamins will fail to thrive, might become ill with acute or chronic illnesses, and likely will be unable to breed. Vitamins are obtained primarily from food, although the body can manufacture certain ones. Humans and birds synthesize some vitamin D from sunlight, and manufacture vitamin K from bacteria in the digestive tract. Research suggests that some species of birds can manufacture vitamin C, but most of the research has been done on poultry, so it's still not clear if this applies to all avian species.

Types of Vitamins

Vitamins are divided into two types, water-soluble and fat-soluble. Fat-soluble vitamins, which include A, D, E, and K, are stored in body tissues, especially in the liver and in body fat. Because they are stored, it is possible (although unlikely) to build up toxic levels of these vitamins. The greatest danger comes from oversupplementing your finch with dietary additives such as cod liver oil, which is extremely high in vitamins A and D. If you do use supplements, please follow the label instructions carefully! The water-soluble vitamins, which include B complex and C, remain in the body for only a short time and must be replenished on a regular basis. Excesses of these vitamins are usually flushed out through the kidneys, so an overdose is highly unlikely.

Vitamin Functions and Sources

✔ Vitamin A: Promotes growth, enhances immune function, and is necessary for the health of eyes, skin, bones, and organs. A deficiency can manifest as dry or flaky skin, eye problems, slow wound healing, or persistent respiratory infections. Vitamin A is available

Millet is a healthy and relatively low-fat grain that is a staple ingredient in finch seed mixes. Whole millet sprays are commonly available, and these are usually coveted treats for Gouldians.

preformed from animal sources as *retinol*, or from plant sources as *beta-carotene*, which the body converts to A. Beta-carotene will not build to toxic levels in tissues, so it is the safest form. Best sources are hard-boiled eggs, cheese, and green or yellow vegetables, including carrots, spinach, broccoli, sweet potatoes, and squash. Seed diets are notoriously deficient in vitamin A.

✔ Vitamin B Complex: Vitamin B is not a single vitamin, but instead is a group of several different B family compounds, including B_1 (thiamine), B_2 (riboflavin), B_3 (niacin), B_6 (pyridoxine), B_{12} (cobalamin), pantothenic acid, biotin, and folic acid. There are between eight and fourteen different compounds in the family, depending on which source you consult. Some compounds, such as choline and inositol, are classed as B vitamins by some sources, but not by others. B complex vitamins serve many functions in the body, including support of metabolism, immune and nervous system functions, and cell growth. A deficiency of any or all of the B complex vitamins can cause anemia, stress, impaired immune function, lack of breeding success, behavioral problems, and poor feathering. Best sources for B vitamins are whole grains (especially wheat germ), brewer's yeast, nuts, legumes, and eggs.

✔ Vitamin C: Vitamin C is a potent antioxidant, and it supports many critical cellular functions. As mentioned earlier, at least some—if not most—birds can produce vitamin C from the glycogen in their liver or kidneys. However, because this vitamin is so critical to health, and the metabolic process has not been heavily researched in exotic birds, I still recommend offering dietary sources of C to your Gouldian. A C deficiency can manifest as bleeding problems, slow wound healing, and suppressed immune function. Good sources of vitamin C for your birds include spinach, broccoli, cabbage, and berries.

✔ Vitamin D: Vitamin D plays a critical role in regulating calcium and phosphorus levels in the blood and organs. Vitamin D is found in two forms: D_2 from plant sources, and D_3 from animal sources. Birds cannot utilize D_2, so you must provide either animal sources such as hard-boiled eggs, or a supplement that contains D_3. Birds can metabolize vitamin D from sunlight, but a captive bird housed indoors will not have that opportunity. Placing the bird's cage near a window does no good—glass and plastic both block the necessary UV rays from penetrating. Without D, your bird cannot properly utilize minerals to build and maintain bone. Deficiency symptoms include soft, deformed, or easily broken bones, soft or thin-shelled eggs, reduced egg production, and seizures or leg weakness. The best food sources of D_3 are fish, dairy products, and fortified cereals. Because it's unlikely your finch will eat these foods, D_3 is best obtained from supplements, such as a good-quality bird multivitamin, or from cod liver oil sprinkled on seed.

✔ Vitamin E: Vitamin E is an antioxidant that supports the reproductive system, skeletal muscles, and the heart and digestive tract. It is known as a "fertility vitamin" due to the role it plays in both male and female fertility, but it also plays a critical role in the immune system, energy production, cardiac health, and some research shows it might even play a role in preventing some cancers. Although it is a fat-soluble vitamin, it is relatively nontoxic even in large doses. Deficiencies usually manifest mostly in breeding birds, and result in poor egg production and decreased hatchability. Extreme deficiencies can cause dystrophy of heart muscle, skeletal muscles, and muscles in the digestive tract. Many seeds and grains are rich in vitamin E. Other good sources are wheat germ, hard-boiled eggs, and leafy green vegetables.

✔ Vitamin K: Vitamin K is essential for normal blood clotting, and it also plays a role in bone formation. Both humans and birds synthesize most of their vitamin K in the digestive tract from beneficial bacteria, so a deficiency in a healthy bird is unlikely. However, certain drugs, including long-term antibiotic treatment, can disrupt the process. A deficiency would cause excessive bleeding from even minor wounds due to the blood's inability to clot. Good dietary sources are leafy green vegetables, alfalfa, kelp, and egg yolks.

Minerals

Minerals are inorganic compounds found in the earth's crust. As such, they can't be manufactured by the body, and must be derived from food. Minerals are first drawn into the food chain mostly by plants, although some animals directly consume minerals from the earth. Examples are the macaws and other parrots that descend on clay licks in South America to eat the mineral-rich red clay. Once in the body, minerals perform a wide variety of functions. There are approximately 22 minerals that are considered essential in the diet, although more than 60 are likely present in the body.

Certain minerals are called macro-minerals because they are needed in relatively large quantities. These include calcium, magnesium, phosphorus, potassium, choline, sodium, and sulfur. Other minerals are necessary to health,

but only in minute quantities. These are referred to as *trace minerals,* and include iron, manganese, copper, iodine, cobalt, and zinc. Gouldians are especially susceptible to iodine deficiencies, which can manifest as a loss of feathering around the bird's head.

Mineral Functions and Sources

✔ Calcium: Calcium is one of the most important and most widely distributed minerals in your bird's body. Calcium is the major building block of bones, and is critical for the transmission of nerve impulses and muscle contraction. Breeding hens have a much higher than normal need for calcium because it is the primary ingredient in eggshell formation. A calcium deficiency can cause weak and easily broken bones, soft-shelled eggs, egg binding, seizures, fainting, and even death. Although many leafy green vegetables contain calcium, some also contain oxalic acid, which binds to calcium and reduces its absorption. Although it's fine to feed greens for all their healthful vitamins, it's also important to provide additional calcium sources such as cuttlebone, crushed oyster shell, or powdered supplements.

✔ Phosphorus: Phosphorus is an important component of bone, and is vital for a host of bodily functions including energy production. Phosphorus is available from most foods, so deficiencies are unlikely. Calcium and phosphorus work together, but your bird requires a calcium/phosphorus ratio of approximately 3:1, so it's important to provide adequate calcium to your pet, especially if it is breeding.

✔ Potassium: Potassium is critical for proper functioning of the heart and kidneys, and works with other minerals to regulate blood pressure and water balance in cells. It's also necessary

Growing chicks have high caloric needs, especially good proteins and fats for proper growth.

for nerve impulses and muscle contraction. Because it is widely available in food, deficiencies are rare. Oranges, bananas, and potatoes are rich sources of potassium. Any excess of this mineral is excreted through the kidneys, so toxicity is also rare.

✔ Magnesium: Magnesium is found primarily in the bone, where it works with calcium and phosphorus. It also influences heart rhythms, so a very low intake could result in cardiac problems. It's abundant in grains, nuts, beans, and leafy vegetables, so a normal bird diet should supply adequate amounts.

✔ Chlorine and Sodium: Chlorine and sodium are found together in sodium chloride, or table salt. These minerals work to maintain the body's acid-base (PH) and fluid balance. Because salt is present in many foods, deficiencies are rare, and the kidneys can excrete excesses up to five or ten times the required amount provided there is sufficient water available.

✔ Sulfur: Sulfur is an essential component of some amino acids, and it is widely available in many organic materials. Good food sources for sulfur include eggs, beans, broccoli, and cabbage.

✔ Iron: Iron is a trace mineral that is critical for the formation of hemoglobin, which carries oxygen in the blood. An iron deficiency causes anemia and weakness. Iron is available from animal or plant sources, but the iron from plants is much harder for the body to utilize. Vitamin C aids in the absorption of iron, and leafy green vegetables are a source of both iron

Calcium and other minerals are important for the health of any bird, but they are especially critical for breeding hens, who must pull calcium from their own bodies to produce eggs.

A varied diet and good eating habits will insure your pet gets all the vital nutrients needed for good health.

Vitamins and other nutrients found in foods are synthesized in the Gouldian's body to produce its beautiful feather colors.

Gouldians can be picky eaters, but a varied diet will help keep your bird healthy and in beautiful feather.

Birds housed outdoors can metabolize vitamin D from sunlight, but indoor birds require full spectrum lighting and supplements.

and C. Other iron sources include eggs, peas, beans, nuts, and dried fruits.

✔ Iodine: Iodine is essential for proper functioning of the thyroid gland and certain other cellular functions. It is found in a variety of foods, but the amount depends on how and where the foods are grown. Deficiencies are rare in most birds, but Gouldians seem to have an above-average need for this trace mineral, and will usually show poor feathering or loss of feathers around the head as the first sign of a deficiency. Fishmeal, cod liver oil, and kelp are all good sources, and dietary iodine supplements are available for cage birds.

✔ Copper: Copper is essential for blood formation, and it keeps bones, blood vessels, and nerves healthy. Copper is abundant in whole grains, so a deficiency is unlikely.

✔ Zinc: Zinc is an important trace mineral that is necessary for cell growth and repair, and for proper functioning of the immune system. Although absolutely critical in small amounts, too much zinc can be toxic. Because of this, some bird fanciers have focused on zinc-plated birdcages and accessories as a potential source of zinc toxicity. You don't have to worry about this for your Gouldians, because finches don't chew on cage wire the way parrots do. However, avoid galvanized dishes, which might indeed transfer high levels of zinc and other metals to your bird's food and water.

Building a Healthy Diet

Because finches are primarily seed-eating birds, the base of your Gouldian's diet should be a high-quality seed mix. Please understand that seed alone is not an adequate diet, but serves as a basic calorie and energy source. In the wild, Gouldians eat a variety of grass seeds and insects. Keep in mind, however, that a captive diet should not necessarily mimic a wild diet, but should improve upon it. Wild birds typically have a shorter life span than captive birds, in part because they can't always forage enough nutrition to prolong their lives.

Seed Varieties and Mixes

Gouldians, like young children, will often choose their favorite foods and eat them to the exclusion of other more healthy items. If this happens, you must still continue to offer a healthy variety so that the birds have the opportunity to eat a well-rounded diet. Sometimes, competition from a cage mate, or perhaps an innate understanding of a looming deficiency, will suddenly jar them into eating in a more balanced manner. Do not ever limit them to just one or two seed types, because "that's all they'll eat." In my experience, birds become malnourished due to imbalanced food offerings, not due to finicky eating.

To begin, choose a high-quality finch or parakeet seed mixture as a base. Most Gouldians show a strong preference for millet seeds and canary grass seed. Don't limit them to just common white proso millet; there are several other types of millet seed available, including red millet, Japanese millet, and small yellow millet. You can find a mix that contains these, or else add some to an existing mix. Many finches also enjoy sterilized hemp seed and Niger (thistle) seed, both of which are oily seeds that add some healthy fat to the diet.

There are also several less common seeds and grains that might appeal to your Gouldians, including steel-cut oats, wheat germ, rapeseed (canola), sesame seed, flax, anise, hulled sunflower pieces, and poppy seeds. Experiment with small quantities of these specialty items and see what your finches enjoy. Keep in mind that the more varied the diet, the more nutrients will be available to your birds.

Sprouted Seeds

Sprouted seeds are an easy way to provide extra nutrition, but if you choose to feed sprouts you must exercise extreme caution. Although sprouts are indeed a highly concentrated source of nutrients, these nutrients and the moisture they require also makes them a wonderful growth medium for all sorts of nasty pathogenic bacteria. In fact, many avian veterinary textbooks now warn against feeding sprouts to birds due to the high probability of contamination. Unfortunately, these pathogens can't be seen, smelled, or detected by the naked eye in any way. Even highly contaminated sprouts can appear fresh and delicious. If you decide to offer sprouts, follow these precautions.

✔ Consider feeding sprouts purchased from the grocery store. Unlike homegrown sprouts, these are grown under strict sanitary controls, and are much less likely to be contaminated.

✔ If you are sprouting at home, wash the seeds carefully before you begin, and rinse the growing sprouts with clean fresh water several times a day. Use only seeds or beans that are meant to be eaten—those that are sold for planting are typically coated with fungicides.

✔ Once the sprouts are growing, place them in the refrigerator. This will slow growth and retard spoiling.

✔ Rinse the sprouts once again before feeding. You can also spray them with one of the many veggie cleaners sold in grocery stores before you rinse them the final time. Handy Pantry

TIP

Spray Millet

Spray millet is a staple food for most Gouldians. It is a relatively low-fat treat that allows the birds to feast and forage in a natural manner. Clip a few sprays to the cage roof, and your birds will cling to it for hours, devouring every last morsel. You can also sprout millet sprays (see Sprouted Seeds, below) to create a more exciting and nutritious treat.

Distributors sells a product called "Sprout Spray" for this very purpose. It's available in many health food stores and produce markets, and uses safe natural ingredients to inhibit mold and bacterial growth.

✔ Remove any uneaten sprouts from the cage after a few hours, even sooner in very warm and humid temperatures.

Green Food

Seed does not provide all the nutrients needed to keep your Gouldians healthy. In order to provide them with all the vitamins and minerals they need, you can offer a variety of fresh greens. Spinach, kale, dark lettuces, beet greens, carrot tops, chickweed, and dandelions are filled with vitamins and should be a welcome treat for your Gouldians. Always wash produce well, and either place it in a dish, or clip it to the cage bars so that your finches can forage naturally.

In fact, you can offer almost any fruit or vegetable to your Gouldians, provided it is washed and chopped to appropriate size. The

Entice your picky eaters with a variety of healthful foods and treats.

exception is avocado, which appears to be toxic to birds. In reality, Goulds tend to be picky eaters, and probably won't embrace every fruit and vegetable you give them, but at least try to get them eating a variety of foods. Try a few sweet offerings, such as finely diced apples, carrots, or chopped grapes. Many birds enjoy fresh corn scraped from the cob. And, as men-

Wild Gouldians consume a lot of insects during the breeding season.

tioned, always remove uneaten produce or other fresh foods after a few hours to prevent poisoning from spoiled foods.

Insects and Other Protein Sources

In the wild, Gouldians eat a variety of insects, especially during breeding season. Bugs are a great source of protein, and play an important role in a healthy diet. You can purchase insect culture foods from supply companies so that you can grow your own, or you can buy live insects at most pet shops. Mealworms are highly favored treats for both birds and reptiles, but they have a hard exoskeleton made of chitin,

which can be difficult to digest. For this reason, limit mealworms to just a few per week. Small crickets, wax worms, and king mealworms (sold as "Superworms") are also healthy treats, and your Gouldian should relish them. If you're squeamish about handling live insects, or are concerned about escapees taking up residence in your home, many pet stores offer dried crickets and other bugs that will work almost as well.

If insects are unwelcome in your home whether dead or alive, then you'll need to provide an alternate protein source. Probably the best way to do this is to offer your birds chopped hard-boiled eggs. You can even leave

══ T I P ══

Weeds

You can gather weeds such as dandelion, chickweed, and clover from your own backyard as a healthy addition to your birds' diet, but always be certain that the weeds haven't been contaminated by herbicides or pesticides. For this reason, stick to your own backyard. You'll have no way of telling if roadside plants have been exposed to dangerous chemicals.

the shell on, which the birds will eat as an excellent source of highly absorbable calcium. Hard-boiled eggs are extremely nutritious, and also make a great vehicle for getting supplements into your Goulds. Simply mash the egg well with vitamin powder or other supplements, and your finches will likely gobble it up. Commercial egg foods that contain powdered egg are also available, and you can use them for convenience.

Supplements

In an ideal world, your Gouldians would get all the nourishment they need from fresh healthy foods; unfortunately, that almost never happens in the real world. Finicky eating, stale foods, stress, and a variety of other factors can prevent your birds from absorbing all the needed nutrients from diet alone. That's where supplements come in handy. Keep in mind that supplements are a wonderful tool to enhance a healthy diet, but they should never be used as a replacement for healthy foods! Following are some of the most common supplements used for cage birds.

Avian vitamin and mineral supplements: These come in a variety of forms, including powders, liquids, and fortified treats. Liquids and some powders are designed to be added to the drinking water, but there are problems inherent in this method. Some of the nutrients, especially the heavier minerals such as calcium, will quickly precipitate to the bottom of the dish and be unavailable to your finch. This method also creates a nutrient-rich soup that can rapidly grow bacteria. And finally, vitamins

In addition to supermarket greens, you can offer your Gouldians a variety of weeds from your backyard. Only pick greens that have not been contaminated by herbicides and pesticides, and wash thoroughly before feeding!

in water lose potency very quickly. If you do go this route, mix the water thoroughly, and replace it twice a day. I recommend adding powdered vitamins to egg food so that the finch gets a more predictable dose.

Probiotics: Probiotics are the healthy bacteria that populate the digestive tract and aid in digestion and vitamin synthesis. In a healthy bird (or animal or human), billions of these bacteria exist in the body, quietly doing their job. Certain factors, such as antibiotic therapy, stress, or infection, can destroy the good bacteria and let unhealthy organisms grow in their place. I always recommend feeding probiotics to birds that are stressed, or to any bird that has been treated with antibiotics. They're also a great supplement for breeding Goulds, and are beneficial to the chicks as well to help them get a good start with a healthy digestive tract. There's no proof that probiotics provide any benefit to healthy adult birds, but they're completely safe and relatively inexpensive, so I do give them to all my birds once or twice a week.

Grit: Grit refers to finely ground minerals that can be soluble, such as ground oyster shell, or insoluble, such as gravel. One of the longest-held myths in aviculture is the belief that finches, canaries, and parrots require insoluble grit to help grind up food in their ventriculus, or muscular stomach. Seed-eating birds that hull seed before swallowing it do not require grit! In fact, ingesting insoluble grit can even be harmful to these birds. Researchers have proven this repeatedly, but still the myth persists. Do not feed gravel to your Gouldians, no matter how many books and articles repeat the fallacy. On the other hand, soluble grit such as ground oyster shell can provide calcium, and the rest will move safely through your bird's

digestive tract. If you have any doubts, consult with your avian veterinarian.

Charcoal: Activated charcoal has been touted as a digestive aid and as a "blood purifier." In veterinary medicine, it's used to pull poisons safely through the digestive tract by preventing their absorption in the gut. Unfortunately, charcoal does the same thing with necessary vitamins and other nutrients. A small bit of charcoal probably won't hurt your finch, but I have yet to see any proof that it provides any actual benefit. Many old-time breeders swear by it, but if you decide to use it, offer it very sparingly.

Powdered kelp or spirulina: These products are derived from dried seaweed (kelp) or algae (spirulina). They're good sources of protein, iodine, and other trace minerals. Because Gouldians are prone to iodine deficiencies, these can be a valuable addition to your Gould's diet. They don't mix well in water, so your best bet is to mix them with mashed hard-boiled eggs as described earlier.

Bee pollen: Some breeders use bee pollen as a high-quality source of protein and trace minerals. Few studies have been done on its effects on birds, but anecdotal reports claim that it enhances their coloring, improves immune response, and stimulates breeding. It is a safe product, so feel free to try it out.

There are many other supplements found on pet store shelves or discussed in Internet chat rooms. Some of these might have nearly magical properties, but others can sicken or even kill your Gouldians. Before you try anything unproven on your birds, talk with your veterinarian or a trusted Gouldian breeder. Remember, good health begins with a healthy diet, and supplements should be used only to fill the gaps.

GOULDIAN FINCH DISEASES AND HEALTH CARE

Nothing shortens a bird's life more than poor living conditions. An inadequate diet, crowded or dirty housing, and unrelenting stress will almost certainly cause life-threatening illness in a captive finch. Sometimes, however, even birds kept in optimal conditions fall ill. That's when your ability to detect and treat problems as soon as they arise can mean the difference between life and death for your Gouldian.

Finding an Avian Veterinarian

The first step in safeguarding your finch's health is to find an avian veterinarian. Avian medicine is much different from dog and cat medicine, so don't expect your regular veterinarian to be a bird expert. You must find a veterinarian who specializes in birds, or at least one who deals with pet birds on a regular basis.

The best way to find a qualified practitioner is to ask other bird people in your area. If you are buying your finch directly from a breeder, he or she can be a valuable source of informa-

Clean cages and a healthy diet will go a long way to keep your Gouldians in tiptop shape.

tion, and will likely have one or more avian veterinarians to recommend. Folks you meet at pet shops and bird fairs might also be able to guide you. Another option is to contact the Association of Avian Veterinarians (AAV) to find the name of a member veterinarian in your area. You can reach the AAV via the Internet at *www.aav.org* or by phone at (561) 393-8901.

Although finding a qualified veterinarian is critical, even the best avian practitioner is useless unless you act promptly when your bird is sick, and then seek the needed care. In time, you will begin to know your bird, and you'll know when it isn't acting normally. We discussed signs of a sick bird in an earlier chapter, but remember that sometimes the symptoms

---

TIP

Check Information

Once you find a qualified avian veterinarian, spend a few minutes exploring his or her policies and fees. Find out how after-hours emergencies are handled, who handles patients when the clinic staff is unavailable, and what tests are recommend for new bird checkups. Some offices will have printed general fee schedules available. Ask if they will accept payment plans for emergencies that arise that are beyond your immediate means. Above all, keep the clinic schedules and contact information in a handy place. You don't want to be frantically rummaging around for telephone numbers when your bird is in acute distress.

---

are subtle and difficult to detect. That is why you must determine what is normal behavior for your finch, and trust your instinct if something doesn't seem right.

Gouldian Finch Diseases

Diseases usually fall into one of five categories: bacterial, viral, fungal, parasitic, or protozoan. As mentioned earlier, quarantining new birds and keeping your finches in clean conditions will help you avoid many opportunistic diseases. But sometimes, despite your best efforts, illness strikes anyway. When it does, always contact your veterinarian for advice. Home treatments with over-the-counter medicines might only worsen the disease and kill

your bird. What follows is a discussion of some of the more common diseases that affect Gouldians, so that you'll have the knowledge you need to talk with your veterinarian and discuss treatment options.

Parasites

Parasites are typically divided into two categories: *ectoparasites*, which live on the outside of the host's body, and *endoparasites*, which live within. Fleas, lice, and mites are ectoparasites; intestinal worms and air sac mites are endoparasites. Some parasites are mostly annoying and can cause stress to your bird, but others are truly life threatening. As with any disease or disorder, it's important to know exactly what you are dealing with before attempting treatment, so always consult your veterinarian.

Air sac mites: Air sac mites (*Sternostoma tracheacolum*) are blood-sucking arthropod endoparasites that are perhaps the number one killer of Gouldians. Recent studies by the Australian government have concluded that air sac mite infections are severely impacting wild populations, causing high death rates and impeding recovery plans. Unfortunately, captive birds are just as prone to respiratory disease from these parasites if they are exposed to other infected birds.

These tiny mites colonize in a bird's trachea (windpipe) and slowly suffocate the host. Contrary to their name, these mites do not always affect the air sacs, which in most birds consist of nine pulmonary sacs that connect to the lungs and provide a huge respiratory capacity. Although they can migrate to any place in the bird's respiratory system, the trachea, especially the area around the syrinx (voice box) is the most common site of infestation. It's sometimes possible to see the mites by wetting down the feathers around the throat and shining a strong light through, which can reveal the presence of tiny dark dots in the trachea.

Symptoms of air sac mites include open-mouthed breathing, coughing, frequent sneezing, nasal discharge, weakness, depression, tail bobbing, and weight loss. An infected bird often makes a characteristic clicking sound as it breathes; experienced finch keepers can tell by the sound that an infestation is present. Infected birds can pass the parasites to other birds by sneezing and coughing, as well as direct contact. Parents transmit the disease to chicks during feeding, and it's likely that contaminated water and feed can be routes of transmission.

There are several treatments available for air sac mites, all with varying degrees of efficacy. In general, drugs that can be administered orally, topically, or by injection are more effective than those that are simply inhaled by the finch. Inhaled treatments, such as No-Pest strips and Sevin (carbaryl) dusting might work for minor infestations, but all too often these methods just drive the mites deeper into the bird's respiratory system. Here's a brief description of accepted treatments:

✔ Ivermectin: Ivermectin can be used orally or topically. In the past, it was sometimes given by injection, but this method is rarely used today due to the stress it places on the bird. For topical use, a 0.1 percent solution (1:10 dilution with propylene glycol) is the most common form. Place a drop of this on the bare skin of the finch's front lower neck, near the jugular vein. Some folks place it under the bird's wing or between the wings on the bird's back. In any case, you might need to gently swab the area with a cotton swab dipped in alcohol to dampen the feathers and find a patch of bare skin. The drug will absorb through the skin and travel through the bird's system, sometimes killing the mites in just one treatment. If not, repeat the treatment every two weeks. Sometimes, resistant mites can take up to six treatments to completely wipe them out. Ivermectin can also be used as an oral medication at the same dosage (1:10 dilution), but when used orally it must be diluted with sterile saline solution, not with propylene glycol. The acceptable dose is one drop (0.05 ml) orally every two weeks for resistant mites. This is a rather high dosage, and some veterinarians prefer to use a more diluted version but give it more frequently. In this case, a dilution of 1:50 is given orally as one drop daily for three or four consecutive days. Keep in mind that Ivermectin is a very powerful drug, and overdoses can be deadly. If your finch appears drowsy or unsteady on its feet after treatment, notify your veterinarian so the dosage can be adjusted.

✔ Moxidectin (SCATT): SCATT is a relatively new product developed in Australia. Like Ivermectin, it is a topical systemic product that is applied to bare skin. Because the life cycle of air sac mites is up to 21 days, any product must either remain in the finch's system for three weeks, or must be readministered until all the mites are dead. SCATT claims to remain in the bloodstream for three weeks, so sometimes only one treatment is necessary.

✔ Carbaryl: Carbaryl powder can be used either topically or as a food additive. When used topically, it is mostly inhaled by the finch, and might not be as effective as a more systemic treatment. Old-time breeders call it the "shake and bake" method. In this treatment, you place 1/4 teaspoon of Sevin dust (0.5 percent carbaryl) into a paper bag, and place your

Finches housed outdoors need shelter from the elements, as well as protection from diseases transmitted by insects and wild birds.

0.05 g of carbaryl with 1 ml of cod liver or olive oil, and then mix the oil with 50 g of seed. Use this treated seed as the only food for two or three days, and repeat the treatment every two weeks, up to three treatments total.

✔ Insecticide strips (dichlorvos): Common household insecticide strips such as the type designed to kill flying insects are sometimes successful at preventing or treating air sac mites. The strip should first be hung outside or otherwise away from the bird for a day or so to dissipate the initial strong concentration of fumes. After that, hang the strip near the birdcage, but far enough away that the bird (and children and other pets) can't reach it. Again, this is most useful in preventing infestations or dealing with very minor outbreaks, but will likely not be effective for severe infestations.

✔ Pyrethrins (Camicide): Pyrethrin-based insecticides such as Camicide are reasonably safe products that are derived from natural chemical compounds in chrysanthemum flowers. Some breeders have had success in eliminating air sac mites by lightly spraying the finch with Camicide once a week.

Feather Mites and Lice: Feather mites and lice include several different species of ectoparasites that live on birds. Finches that live outside are most at risk due to possible transmission from wild birds. Most of these parasites are not host-specific, which means that feather mites or lice from other species of birds can infest your Gouldian. Although these parasites are not life-threatening by themselves, they can cause your finch so much discomfort and stress that it will succumb to stress-related disease. An infested finch might not be able to sleep, can lose its appetite, and will generally be miserable. Signs of infestation in your bird can

Gouldian into the bag. Hold the bag closed for 30 seconds, and shake or tap it gently. As the bird flutters in the bag, it will inhale the dust and be coated with a light powdering. Release it immediately back into its cage. This can work on minor infestations, but the mites sometimes just move deeper into the respiratory tract to escape the poison. As a food additive, mix include extreme restlessness, excessive preening or biting at its feathers, poor feathering or bald patches. One species, *Knemidokoptes pilae* (scaly mites), causes hyperkeratotic lesions (skin growths) on the face, feet, and sometimes around the cloaca.

Another genera commonly known as quill mites burrow directly into the feather shaft, causing extreme discomfort to the bird. It's not usually necessary to determine exactly what species of mite or lice is causing the problem, because the treatment is the same.

Treatment for external parasites is much the same as treatments described for air sac mites: pyrethrins or carbaryl for average outbreaks, or Ivermectin for more severe or resistant infestations. However, I do not recommend the various clip-on mite and lice defenders that are made to be attached to the cage. Most of these contain paradichlorobenzene, the chemical that is commonly found in mothballs. Studies have shown that it is a probable carcinogen. Inhaling the fumes can cause dizziness, headaches, and nausea in humans, and high doses are toxic. Stick to the treatments described, which have a long history of relatively safe use in birds.

Worms: Worms, like feather mites, are primarily a threat to birds housed outdoors. If you house your Gouldian inside, you probably won't have to deal with worming. If your bird was bred in outdoor aviaries or is kept outdoors even briefly, however, it could possibly be infected. Worms are mostly spread when a bird ingests worm eggs from contaminated soil or insects. For example, tapeworms (*Cestodes*) and gizzard worms (*Spiruroid*) use insects as intermediate hosts. During breeding seasons, Gouldians often turn to insects as a protein source for their young, and are thus infected. Round-

Bengalese (Society) finches make wonderful foster parents for Gouldians, but they can be latent carriers of **Cochlosoma** *protozoa.*

worms (*Ascaridia*) and threadworms (*Capillaria*) can be transmitted in soil infected by wild bird droppings or earthworms. Most intestinal worms cause symptoms such as weight loss, anorexia, anemia, diarrhea, and general poor health. Treatment depends on the type of worm present. Some breeders will routinely dose their birds with worming medications once or twice a year, but this "shotgun approach" might not be helpful if the medication they are using is ineffective against the type of worm present. In most cases, your veterinarian can identify the culprit through simple fecal tests or swabs, and then prescribe the most effective treatment.

Protozoan Infections

Protozoa are microscopic one-celled animals that colonize inside your bird and can cause serious disease. There are numerous species of protozoa, but there are a few that are likely to cause disease in cage birds. The most common are as follows:

Cochlosoma: Cochlosoma (*Cochlosoma spp.*) is a flagellate (whiplike) organism that inhabits the gastrointestinal tract, causing dehydration and an inability to digest food. Bengalese (Society) finches are often latent carriers, and when they are used as foster parents they can pass the disease on to Gouldian chicks. This organism is especially fatal to nestlings, and can cause high mortality in an aviary. Treatment with ronidazole is usually effective. The dosage is 400 mg mixed with each kilogram of egg food, along with 400 mg mixed with one liter of water and used as drinking water for five days. After a two-day rest and return to nonmedicated food and water, the treatment should be repeated.

Coccidiosis: Protozoa belonging to the *Isospora spp., Eimeria spp.,* or *Atoxoplasma* genus usually cause Coccidia infections in finches. These infections are rare in indoor birds, but can affect finches housed outdoors. Those birds with access to the ground are especially at risk, because the protozoa complete a portion of their life cycle in the ground, where birds or insects then ingest them. Some infected birds can remain asymptomatic, but those that are stressed or overcrowded can develop bloody or mucus-filled diarrhea, dehydration, and anemia. Trimethoprim-sulfa medication is the treatment of choice.

Trichomonas: *Trichomonas spp.* infections are commonly referred to as *canker*. It's a very common disease in wild pigeons and doves, and can affect finches housed outdoors. These protozoa usually infect the esophagus and crop (sometimes the liver), and can cause symptoms such as gagging, regurgitation, neck stretching, and green diarrhea. In some cases, white or yellowish plaques are visible in the bird's mouth. Treatment is usually oral metronidazole, sometimes accompanied by antibiotics.

Fungal Diseases

Although there are many different types of disease-causing fungi, there are two that commonly cause illness in finches: *Candida albicans,* and *Aspergillus spp.*

Candida: Candida is most common in chicks, but can affect adults as well. It is usually associated with a suppression of the immune system, and in adult birds it commonly occurs when antibiotic therapy wipes out the "good bacteria" that is normal in a bird's digestive tract. That is why veterinarians often prescribe antifungals along with antibiotics when the planned course of treatment is lengthy. Chicks are predisposed because they have not yet built up a strong immune system and the necessary healthy bacteria. If the normal gut flora is disturbed for any reason, then this opportunistic yeast can colonize, especially in the crop and esophagus. Symptoms include vomiting and weight loss in all ages, and thickened or slow crop in chicks. In some cases, whitish plaque that looks like cottage cheese is visible in the mouth. Candida usually responds well to nystatin, an antifungal drug that is safe even on young chicks. I also recommend adding some healthy bacteria (known commonly as probiotics) into the bird's diet. There are several good brands on the market, including Bene-Bac powder or gel and Ornabac powder.

Aspergillosis: *Aspergillus spp.* cause a much more serious disease known as aspergillosis, sometimes referred to simply as "asper." These fungi are found throughout the environment, and usually don't cause much trouble. However, if a bird is stressed, malnourished, has a compromised immune system, or is kept in dirty conditions, then aspergillosis can develop. Moldy or musty seed and bedding are common sources of the fungi. Asper, like many other bird diseases, is far easier to prevent than it is to treat. If you keep your Gouldian's cage clean, feed only fresh seed, and keep the water dish fresh and clean, then you will likely never have to deal with aspergillosis. Symptoms of the disease include respiratory difficulties, weight loss, and sometimes diarrhea. The bird might shake its head or stretch its neck and gape as if it is choking. It is a very difficult disease to treat, especially in small birds such as finches. Lengthy treatments that include nebulizing the birds with drugs such as amphotericin B are sometimes successful in parrots, but rarely in Gouldians.

Bacterial Diseases

There are many different types of bacteria; some are harmful, even lethal, but others are actually necessary for normal body processes. Every day, the "good" bacteria in the body work to crowd out the harmful invaders. When something upsets this delicate balance, the dangerous pathogens can take over, and cause illness.

Bacteria are usually divided into two types: gram-negative, and gram-positive. In very general terms, gram-positive bacteria are typically harmless and normal for your bird, but gram-negative can cause illness. This is an oversimpli-

fication, and there are exceptions, but most of the usual bacterial infections in cage birds are caused by various gram-negative species.

Enterobacter: The most common are *Enterobacteriaceae,* which includes many different gram-negative bacteria that usually attack the gastrointestinal tract and can cause severe illness, organ damage, and death. The most common of these is *Escherichia coli. E. coli* exists in several different strains. Some are commonly found in the digestive tract of humans and other mammals, and usually cause them no harm. More virulent strains have been implicated in human deaths and disease outbreaks across the country, primarily from consuming undercooked meat that has been contaminated with the bacteria. *E. coli* is not normal digestive flora for finches, however, and any form of it can cause illness in your Gouldians.

Symptoms of *E. coli* infection include lethargy, loss of appetite, and diarrhea. If the bird isn't treated promptly with appropriate

Chicks are very susceptible to Candida *fungus, but it can affect adult birds as well.*

antibiotics, the infection will usually attack the kidneys or liver and cause death. By the time you see visible symptoms, your finch is critically ill and must receive immediate treatment if it is to survive.

Chicks are very susceptible to Candida *fungus, but it can affect adult birds as well.*

Salmonella: *Salmonella spp.* are another common but dangerous group of enterobacter bacteria that can attack your Goulds. Symptoms of *Salmonella* are similar to that of *E. coli*, but severe or chronic infections can also manifest as central nervous system problems, arthritis, joint pain, and even conjunctivitis (red irritated eyes). *Salmonella* is especially difficult to treat because it can exist in a subclinical carrier state in birds that appear completely healthy. These birds can pass it on to others, including immunosuppressed humans who come in contact with infected droppings. Certain forms of the bacteria can even be passed from the hen into her eggs, and is a likely suspect in dead-in-shell eggs. *Salmonella* can sometimes be difficult to eradicate, so always work with a veterinarian to develop effective treatment protocols.

Chlamydia: *Chlamydia psittaci* is a bacterium that causes severe or chronic disease in many species of birds. It is most common in parrots, where it is known as psittacosis or "parrot fever." It can, however, infect Gouldians, especially those that come in contact with parrots. When the infection affects birds other than parrots, it is referred to as ornithosis or chlamydiosis. Despite the different names, they are all the same disease from the same bacterium. Chlamydiosis is a zoonotic disease, which means that it can be transmitted to humans (and other animals). In humans, it causes mild to moderate flu-like symptoms, although it rarely affects

Experienced finch keepers can sometimes diagnose air sac mites based on the clicking sounds an infected bird makes as it breathes.

Quarantine sick birds away from the rest of your flock to discourage disease transmission.

healthy adults. Elderly or immunosuppressed people are most at risk, but the infection in humans usually responds quickly to antibiotics.

In birds, however, the infection can be subclinical in carrier birds, or can cause severe disease and death in susceptible individuals. Symptoms include lethargy, depression, dehydration, weight loss, green or yellow urates, difficulty breathing, and sinusitis. If left untreated, the bird will die.

Antibiotic therapy can be effective, but the treatment must continue for at least 45 days.

Although the above types of infection are the most common, there are dozens of other species of bacteria that can sicken your Gouldians, and they will often cause similar symptoms. You will not be able to tell what kind of bacteria is responsible just by evaluating the symptoms. The only accurate way to diagnose the problem is by having your veterinarian culture the infected bird's droppings or other body fluids to find out exactly what is growing, and what antibiotic would be most effective. If the finch is very ill and time is of the essence, your veterinarian will likely prescribe a broad-spectrum antibiotic that is effective against many different strains of bacteria.

And, as always, the best treatment is prevention. Bacteria multiply best in unclean conditions, and insects and rodents will transfer the germs from one area to another. Sometimes, just keeping your birds clean is all it takes to prevent bacterial outbreaks.

Viruses

There are dozens of viruses that can infect Gouldians, but most of them are pretty rare in captivity. The best way to avoid viral diseases in your birds is to carefully quarantine any new arrivals. Keep in mind that if you keep your Goulds outdoors, they will be susceptible to viruses transmitted by wild birds. Viruses can't be treated with antibiotics, although your veterinarian might prescribe them to fight off any secondary opportunistic infections that can attack an already weakened finch.

In general, viruses are treated by prescribing medications to alleviate the symptoms, while the bird's immune system works to clear the active infection. In addition to providing supportive care, you'll need to keep the sick finch away from all other birds to prevent the virus from spreading. Many (but not all) viruses are highly contagious, so quarantine sick birds and clean the cages thoroughly! Some of the more common viruses are described below.

Polyomavirus: Polyomavirus usually causes lethal infections in nestlings, and typically less severe disease in adults. Unfortunately, adult birds can be asymptomatic carriers of the virus. Gouldian chicks that are exposed to the disease can die within a few days of hatching. Those that survive will display poor feathering, retarded growth, and occasionally a deformed lower mandible that grows long and tubular. There is currently no treatment for polyomavirus.

Poxvirus: Poxvirus can be transmitted by mosquitoes and mites, and it is often fatal. Infected birds may be lethargic or have difficulty breathing shortly before death. In less severe infections, the finch will develop lesions, tearing, and crustiness around the eyes. Although there is no treatment for the virus, supportive care, including antibiotics to prevent secondary infection, can help a bird survive. Sometimes extra vitamin A helps to heal the lesions. Recovered birds might, however, become carriers of the virus.

Paramyxovirus: Paramyxovirus exists in three different forms that can infect a wide variety of avian species. The type that most commonly affects Gouldians typically manifests as central nervous system symptoms, including tremors and paralysis, but it can also display as weight loss, yellowish diarrhea, and conjunctivitis.

Cytomegalovirus: Cytomegalovirus is a type of herpes virus that is highly fatal to Gouldians. In one outbreak in Europe, about 70 percent of exposed birds died. Symptoms include depression, loss of appetite, conjunctivitis, and labored breathing. It is not widely reported in the United States.

Although some viruses are relatively stable in the environment, others are fragile and don't live long outside the host. If you are experiencing a viral outbreak, always discuss environmental control with your veterinarian. A careful regimen of cleaning and disinfecting will help destroy many viruses and slow down or prevent new infections.

Other Diseases and Disorders

Sometimes birds become ill and we can't identify any infectious agents. There are a few such disorders common to Gouldians. Some are likely related to poor diet or husbandry, although others might be due to disease processes that haven't yet been identified. As you've probably noticed throughout this chapter, a wide variety of diseases display the same set of symptoms, so it's critical to consult with your veterinarian for a proper diagnosis. Even if you can't reach a definitive diagnosis, you'll at least be prepared to treat the symptoms in the most effective manner.

Twirling Syndrome

Twirling syndrome is the name given to a collection of neurological symptoms sometimes displayed by Gouldians, especially those that have been recently shipped to a new home. Symptoms include torticollis (spasms of the neck muscle that cause the head to be twisted sideways or upside down), inability to perch, and spinning in circles. About 20 percent of affected birds die, and those that recover may exhibit a permanent head tilt and balance problems.

Researchers suspect a virus, most likely a Paramyxovirus, causes this syndrome, but to date they haven't conclusively identified the cause. Other theories are that it relates to a genetic defect, a damaged eardrum, or nutritional deficiencies. Although it's possible that all of these factors contribute to the syndrome, a transient virus is the most likely culprit. Antibiotics have been of no use in treating the syndrome, except in cases where a secondary bacterial infection is worsening the problem. In any case, offering supportive care and adding vitamin supplements to the diet might help your Gouldian recover from this disorder.

Star-Gazing

Star-gazing refers to a condition in which the Gouldian tips its head backward so that its head rests on its back. In mild and transient cases, it could be a behavioral response from being placed in a too-small or unfamiliar cage. When the posture is frequent or severe, it most likely indicates a neurological problem. A deficiency of thiamine (vitamin B_1) can cause star-gazing, and many cases clear up within hours of vitamin B_1 therapy. Even when a thiamine deficiency isn't the cause of the disorder, it can be a helpful supplement for treating almost any neurological problems.

Egg Binding

Egg binding refers to a condition in which female birds are unable to properly expel an egg. In some cases, the eggshell is soft or incomplete and can't be expelled with normal muscle contractions. In other cases, the egg is normal, but the muscle contractions are weak. There are dozens of different causes and contributing factors, but when egg binding occurs it is a serious threat to the hen's life.

An egg-bound hen will appear weak and depressed. She will usually stand with a wide-legged stance, and might wag her tail or show other visible signs of straining. She will be reluctant or unable to fly or perch, and might

Black-headed/white-breasted male.

display lameness or paralysis in her legs. In the very early stages of egg binding, sometimes just supplying extra heat and humidity is enough to help her pass the egg. You can also deposit a drop of water-soluble lubricant such as KY jelly into her cloaca. Mineral oil or olive oil will also work in a pinch, but will ruin the egg. If these measures don't work within an hour or so, or if her condition appears to be deteriorating, you must get her to a veterinarian immediately. A veterinarian can administer various drugs or injectible vitamins to increase contractions. If all those methods fail, the egg will need to be extracted from the oviduct.

Egg binding is usually easier to prevent than it is to treat. In most cases, it's caused by poor nutrition, although environmental factors such as lack of proper humidity can contribute. Very young hens are more prone to egg binding, so please don't allow youngsters to breed!

Normal red-headed male.

Heat

If your Gouldian becomes ill, there are some important steps you can take to help it survive. The single most important thing that a sick bird requires is heat. The bird will not have the strength to maintain its body heat and to fight off the invading disease at the same time. If you can help keep it warm, it can turn all its resources to its immune system.

Hospital Cage

The best way to keep your finch warm is to place it in a hospital cage. To devise a homemade version, you'll need the following supplies.

- A small glass aquarium
- Screen cover to fit the aquarium top
- Heating pad with low, medium, and high settings
- Heavy towel
- Stick-on thermometer, commonly sold in pet stores for reptile tanks
- Small food and water crocks
- A portable perch or piece of sanitized driftwood sold for reptiles
- Paper towels

Lay the heating pad on a counter or heat-resistant surface, and set the heat to low. Place the aquarium on top of the heating pad so that the pad covers about half of the aquarium bottom. Line the bottom of the tank with paper towels, and place the perch and food and water dishes inside. If you can't find portable perches, a piece of driftwood or other woods typically sold for reptile enclosures will allow your finch to sit above the aquarium floor and give it a sense of security. Next, affix the thermometer to the front of the aquarium glass on the half that is not over the heating pad. You can now place your Gouldian inside the tank, put on the screen cover, and drape a towel across the top half of the tank that is sitting on the heating pad. The towel will help to hold in heat and humidity, and will also allow the bird to rest without distractions.

Temperature

You'll want to keep the temperature between 85 and 90°F (29–32°C). If necessary, turn the heating pad to medium setting. If it's too warm, pull the towel back a bit to allow more heat to escape, and reduce heat to low setting.

Humidity

If you're dealing with an egg-bound hen or a bird in respiratory distress, the next step is to add humidity. The rate at which water evaporates and creates humidity is based on the surface area of water; therefore, a wide shallow crock will provide more

A homemade hospital cage will supply much needed warmth to your finch while it recuperates. Sick birds expend a great deal of energy trying to keep their body temperatures up.

GOULDIAN

humidity than a tall narrow jar. A shallow crock is also a better choice because it won't create a drowning hazard for a weak or disoriented finch. You can enhance evaporation even more by placing a clean sponge in the crock, then filling it with water level with the top of the sponge. The irregular surface of the sponge exposes more surface area to the air, and thus humidifies better than water alone.

Oral drugs can be dripped carefully into a sick finch's mouth to administer exact dosages.

Traveling to the Veterinarian

Once your finch is settled into the hospital cage, contact your veterinarian. Without appropriate medications, your Gould probably won't survive. If you must travel with a sick bird, you can carry it in the same aquarium used as a hospital cage, but remove the water dishes during transit. Be certain the screen top is on securely, and cover it with a towel to hold in the heat and calm the finch. Fasten the tank securely with a seat belt so sudden stops don't cause it to tip over.

Administering Medications

If your veterinarian prescribes medication, it might come in several forms. Drugs that are added to the bird's food or water are the easiest to administer, but unfortunately aren't always the most effective—because the dosage is dependent on how much the finch drinks or eats, it's difficult to get an exact dose. The sickest Gouldians might lose their appetites and refuse to eat or drink, thereby not getting enough medicine to cure the illness. If you have a large number of finches that require medication, however, dosing the food or water might be the only practical solution.

Topical drugs are usually applied to a patch of bare skin on the Gouldian's body, and are then absorbed into the bloodstream. These can be very effective, but only certain drugs (mostly antiparasitics) are available in this form.

Injectible medications are the most precise, and usually the fastest-acting. Unfortunately, they're also very stressful for a bird as tiny as a Gouldian, and require some skill to perform the injections. If you're comfortable administering drugs in this manner, your veterinarian will be able to demonstrate the proper method and supply the correct syringes.

Oral medications, like injectibles, allow you to get a precise dosage into the bird. You can use a small syringe (without needle) or an eyedropper. Hold the finch gently, being careful not to squeeze its chest and restrict its breathing. Place the tip of the eyedropper into its mouth, and carefully dispense the medicine toward the rear of the mouth on the bird's right side. This directs it toward the esophagus, and not the trachea (windpipe).

Caution: When giving any medication, measure the dosage and follow instructions carefully!

While your Gouldian is recuperating in the hospital cage, take this opportunity to thoroughly clean and disinfect its cage and the surrounding area. If you have other birds (of any species) in the house, keep the sick bird as far away from them as possible to stop the infection from spreading.

BREEDING GOULDIAN FINCHES

As you gain experience in keeping Gouldians, you might decide to try breeding your finches. Sometimes you wind up with opposite-sex pairs, and the birds begin a breeding program of their own, without any input from you! In either case, your knowledge and husbandry techniques will greatly impact the number of live and healthy chicks produced.

In the wild, Gouldians breed during the wet season, when days are longest and seed grasses and insects peak. The gradually increasing daylight and torrential rainfall cause the dry savannas and grasslands to spring to life, bringing abundant food and water to the furred and feathered inhabitants. It is then that birds begin to nest, knowing that the bounty of the land will provide them with plenty of food to raise their chicks.

In captivity, food should always be abundant, so captive Gouldians can and will nest at any time during the year. Increasing light, either natural or artificial, might stimulate those that are slow starters. Therefore, finches housed out-

Breeding your finches can be a rewarding hobby.

doors are most likely to begin breeding in spring or early summer, and indoor breeders can be encouraged (or discouraged) to breed at any time of the year through manipulation of aviary lighting. Indoor birds frequently go to nest in the fall, perhaps because the aviculturist unintentionally extends the day length through increased use of artificial lighting.

The Basics

To begin with, it's important to have a compatible and healthy pair of birds. Because Gouldians are dimorphic, which means that males and females are visibly different, it's easy to determine sex once the birds have molted into adult coloring. To choose a pair of birds for breeding, consider the following:

✔ Are they the proper age? Gouldians can begin producing as early as six months of age, but you should never attempt to breed birds that young. Very young birds usually make poor parents, and can experience a greater variety of health problems, including egg binding and soft-shelled eggs. Wait until they're at least one year old before setting them up in a breeding program, perhaps even closer to two years. On the other hand, be certain the Goulds you are buying are not past their prime. Ideally, they should be under three years of age when you purchase them so that they have a few reproductive years left.

✔ What are their genetics? If you are interested in breeding certain colors, you must have a clear understanding of the genetic background of the birds you're purchasing. Even if you're simply raising the finches for pleasure and don't care what color chicks you wind up with, future purchasers will likely want this information, so ask questions of the seller and keep clear records.

✔ Are they healthy? See page 18 for information on choosing a bird. Begin with a good pair, and then offer them the best food and care to strengthen them further. Producing and rearing chicks is extremely demanding on the parents, especially on the hen. A weak female might attempt to reproduce, but with disastrous results to her own health, and to the health of her chicks.

✔ Do they like each other? Unlike dogs and cats, Gouldians are monogamous, and must feel some attraction or affection for each other or they won't breed. We'll discuss mating rituals a little later in this chapter, but never purchase a pair of birds that actively avoid each other, fight, or appear frightened of one another. If you spot a pair perching near each other or verbalizing back and forth, it's likely they'll get along just fine.

The Breeding Cage

Gouldians typically breed better in indoor cages than they do in outdoor flights, so the information about choosing a cage on pages 29–30 applies to breeding cages as well. As always, your birds will enjoy the longest cage possible, preferably 36 to 40 inches (91–102 cm) in length.

Box Cage

Some Goulds prefer a box cage for breeding. A box cage is constructed of wood on all sides, except for a wire front. This type of cage gives them shelter and privacy; if you're handy, you can build one yourself for very little money. Of course, you can also mimic the box cage design by draping the existing cage on three sides with heavy fabric during the breeding season. The fabric is easy to wash, and will save you the time and expense of specially constructed breeding cages.

Nest Boxes

In the wild, Gouldians are cavity nesters, much like parrots and woodpeckers. They will choose a hole in a tree that has rotted out or has been excavated by another species. Sometimes they'll even nest in termite mounds. This means that their nests are dark and covered, as opposed to the open woven nests of many other songbirds.

In captivity, they will much prefer a wooden nest box like the type used to breed budgies and lovebirds. A typical budgie nest box is approximately 6 inches long by 8 inches wide by 8 inches tall (16 × 20 × 20 cm), and will work just fine. A slightly smaller size will work too, but don't go much larger or the finches might feel it's too large. You can hang the nest box either inside or outside of the cage, as long as you can easily access it for candling eggs or checking on the chicks. Be sure to offer the birds suitable nesting material. Most pet stores sell a variety, including coconut fibers, clean hay, and several other fibers designed for nesting birds. Gouldians aren't particularly talented nest builders, but they should as least drag some material into the box to cushion the eggs. You can also give them a start by tossing in a handful yourself.

Breeding Diets

If you've been feeding your pair a wholesome diet filled with a variety of foods, you won't need to change the diet a great deal to enhance breeding. In general, a breeding diet must be higher in protein and fat than a maintenance diet, and must provide adequate calcium. A typical maintenance diet is usually about 10 to 14 percent protein, and 4 to 6 percent fat. A breeding diet should provide protein levels of 18 to 20 percent, and fat levels of approximately 8 percent. You can achieve this relatively simply by offering more insects and egg food, and adding a daily calcium supplement to the food. There are also several excellent breeder supplement foods on the market. You can experiment to see which ones your birds prefer.

Note: As the birds move into breeding condition, you'll probably see a change in their beak color. Typically, the male's beak brightens to a pearly white, while the hen's beak darkens to a grayish black.

Unfortunately, if your Gouldians are picky eaters and haven't been eating well, attempting to breed them will only exacerbate any nutritional deficiencies. Do not encourage breeding in birds on a marginal diet! They will not be strong enough, and you will risk their health, especially that of the hen. An egg-laying hen must replace her total blood plasma calcium approximately every fifteen minutes during the period of egg calcification. If she doesn't have sufficient stores of this mineral, her body will attempt to pull too much from her bones and blood plasma, which can result in a multitude of physical problems, up to and including the hen's death.

The Mating Ritual

When a male is interested in breeding, he will court the hen with elaborate displays of song and dance. If the hen is interested, she'll sit near the male and watch him strut and sing. According to researchers, Gouldians produce one of the most complex songs of all songbirds, consisting of three unrelated harmonics. During the song, the male will puff out his mask and breast feathers, hop, and toss his head from side to side. Frequently, he'll bend down toward the perch and then toss his head back and assume a stiff vertical posture, all the while singing his heart out.

If the hen is likewise inclined toward the male, she'll move closer to him, bow down, and quiver her tail. She might also sing softly in answer to his calls. Depending on the pair, this display can go on for quite a while. The actual mating process usually takes place in the nest box due to the Gould's extremely shy nature. Both birds might carry nesting material into the box, but the male is the prime architect.

Draping three sides of the cage with heavy fabric will give the breeding pair and their chicks some welcome privacy.

An eight-day-old chick shows little of the beauty it will display when it matures.

An interested hen will sit close to the male and watch his courtship display intently.

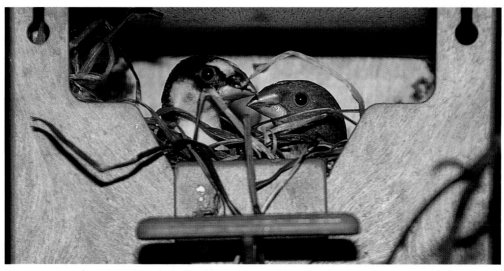

If you are serious about breeding Gouldians, you might consider keeping a pair of Bengalese (Society) finches as well. They make excellent foster parents if you find yourself dealing with inexperienced or unwilling Gouldian parents.

Egg Laying and Incubation

Once the birds have begun to mate in earnest, the hen will begin to visit the nest box more frequently. The first egg usually appears within a week, and she'll lay another each day until the clutch is complete. Gouldians can produce up to eight eggs, but five or six is a more average clutch size. Most hens don't begin to incubate until the clutch is nearly complete. Because of this, the chicks often hatch all on the same day.

The normal incubation period is 14 to 15 days, and both parents share the task. Usually the hen broods the eggs at night while the male stands guard, but during the day they take turns. Sometimes both birds will sit together in the nest to keep one another company.

Candling

After about five days of incubation, you'll be able to tell if the eggs are fertile by candling them. You can use a small, powerful flashlight, but I highly recommend that you purchase a flexible candling light designed to inspect eggs without removing them from the nest. These are inexpensive, and the bulb is recessed so that it doesn't generate a lot of heat, which might kill or injure the developing embryo. If you use a flashlight, you'll need to remove the eggs to inspect them. Always wash and dry your hands thoroughly so that you don't introduce any pathogens, and use a clean tissue to handle the eggs, because human skin oils can clog the delicate pores of the shell. Handle them with extreme care! Rough movements can jar and kill the growing chick, especially during early stages of growth.

Carefully place the flashlight or candling light against the egg. If it is fertile, you'll be able to see a profusion of tiny red veins snaking away from a small central dot that is the growing embryo. Infertile eggs will simply display a yellowish glow from the yolk. These veins aren't visible until several days after incubation commences, so be certain that the hen has been incubating before you decide the eggs are infertile. I usually return them to the nest and check again in a few days before I remove and discard them.

If you do discard infertile eggs, the pair will usually go back to nest rather quickly. If, however, the second clutch is infertile, you should remove the nest box and allow the birds to rest. Review their diet and be certain they aren't carrying subclinical disease before you let them try again. Sometimes, young and inexperienced finches take a few tries before they get it right, but make sure inexperience is the only problem they're dealing with.

Hatchlings

If all goes according to plan, the chicks should begin arriving in about two weeks. You might notice a difference in the parents' behavior shortly before hatching. Sometimes, both parents will refuse to leave the box, or the male might jump in and out of the box, calling excitedly to his mate. Chicks typically hatch in the morning, and emerge from the egg blind, naked, helpless, and exhausted. They will probably begin begging for food after a brief resting period. Don't be concerned if the parents don't begin feeding them immediately. Shortly before a chick hatches, it must absorb the yolk sac into its body. The remaining absorbed yolk will provide nourishment for the new hatchling for several hours, perhaps longer.

Once chicks are imminent, be certain to provide the parents with plenty of soft food to feed the chicks, and replace it frequently so that it doesn't grow nasty bacteria. There are several good-quality commercial nestling foods on the market, and you can feed these plain or mixed with a mashed hard-boiled egg. If the parents will accept insects, now is the time to provide them. Chicks need a lot of protein and fat to grow properly, and they'll never make it on a seed-only diet.

Society Finches

Unfortunately, not all Gouldians are good parents. Certain adults will refuse to feed the nestlings, or will throw healthy chicks from the nest. This is most common in young, inexperienced pairs, but some Gouldians never seem to get the hang of parenthood. In those cases, many Gouldian breeders use Society (Bengalese) finches as foster parents.

If you're serious about breeding Gouldians, you should consider keeping a few breeding pairs of Society finches as well. Societies are usually wonderful parents, and will gladly accept Gouldian eggs if they're placed in the nest while the Society hen is brooding. You will have to remove the Society eggs, and perhaps foster them under another pair. It's not usually a good idea to mix clutches, but some folks have had success doing so. The most important factor is the age of the chicks. If there is more than a two- or three-day difference in the age of the Society chicks and the Gouldian chicks, the smaller babies will not get fed properly, and will perish.

Leaving the Nest

Gouldian chicks grow rapidly, and should be fully feathered and ready to leave the nest in

TIP

Nodules

An interesting thing that you might notice about Gouldian chicks is the luminous blue papillae (nodules) that are placed at the rear beak margins. These reflective patches, along with mouth and beak markings, allow the parent birds to properly place the food into a chick's mouth in a darkened nesting hole. The papillae don't emit light, but they will reflect even minute amounts of ambient light, and will give the chick's mouth a "glow-in-the-dark" appearance. That insures that mom or dad don't miss stuffing food into the hungry mouths.

about 21 days. At this age, they'll still be clumsy and probably unwilling to eat entirely on their own. They'll chase the parents, especially the father, all over the cage, begging to be fed. After a few days, most youngsters will finally begin to feed themselves. Make sure you have plenty of food available so that the babies learn good eating habits from the start. You can move the youngster to a cage of their own when they're five or six weeks old, sooner if the parents get annoyed and start to pick on them.

Banding

As mentioned earlier, closed leg bands are important if you wish to accurately track your Goulds and document a bird's pedigree. You can obtain closed bands from many organizations and avicultural suppliers. Two good sources are

A nestling finch with clearly visible beak papillae.

Be certain that chicks are independent and eating well before you send them to a new home.

Hand-feeding and handling the chicks will help tame and help them lose their innate fear of humans.

Always begin your breeding program with healthy birds from known bloodlines.

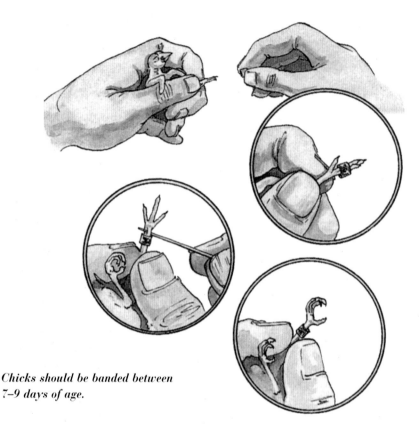

Chicks should be banded between 7–9 days of age.

the American Federation of Aviculture, on the web at *www.afabirds.org* and L&M Bird Leg Bands in San Bernadino, California, telephone 909-882-4649.

Gouldian chicks should be banded when they are between seven and nine days old. To do so:

1. Thoroughly wash and dry your hands, and then remove the chick from the nest.

2. Gently bunch together the front three toes, and slide the band carefully over the toes and foot, and onto the chick's ankle.

3. At this point, the chick's rear toe is probably trapped under the band. Gently work the

toe free using your fingers, or else slide a toothpick between the bird's trapped toe and ankle, and gently wiggle the toe free. When you are done, the band should rest easily on the baby's ankle.

4. Be certain to write down the identifying band number and any pertinent information, and return the chick to the nest.

5. If you wait too long and the band won't fit over the foot, do not ever attempt to force it on or you can severely injure the chick. If it's just a little snug, you can dab a bit of soap or oil onto the foot to ease the band on, but if it still won't slide on easily, then quit. You can purchase open bands that are placed on the leg of an adult bird by using a special tool. Although closed bands are the preferred method of marking, please don't risk damaging a chick's leg in an effort to force on the band.

Record Keeping

If you are serious about breeding your Gouldians, then careful record keeping is a must. Other breeders are most likely seeking a specific genetic type, and won't be interested in purchasing chicks with an undocumented bloodline. Even if you just intend to sell them as pets, the new pet owner might someday decide to breed the birds, and will appreciate knowing the parentage.

Although keeping records is important, how you keep them is a matter of choice. There are several good computer programs on the market that allow you to document pairs, their offspring, keep track of health issues and veterinary visits, and so on. If you don't wish to go the high-tech route, a spiral bound notebook or index card system will work just fine.

Begin with a master record for each breeding bird, which should include information, such as age, gender, band number, genetic makeup, breeding history, where you obtained the bird, and any health issues or vet visits. Link the master records together for each pair, either by band number or name. Once the pair goes to nest, keep a record of dates the eggs are laid, clutch sizes, hatch dates, and any other notes that will be helpful to you in the future.

When you band the chicks, prepare a new master record for each bird you band. Note the

chick's visual color and sex, and the known genetics of the parent birds. You should keep copies of these records for yourself, and also provide a copy to the new owners as you sell the youngsters.

Raising Gouldians is both a challenge and a pleasure, and you will most likely find it a very rewarding pastime. If you are serious about the hobby, make the effort to search out literature and organizations such as breeder clubs that can help expand your knowledge. Your birds will benefit from your knowledge, and will likely reward you with many broods of happy and healthy chicks.

GOULDIAN FINCH GENETICS

As we discussed in the first chapter, wild Gouldians can display either red, black, or yellow (orange) head coloring. If you're serious about breeding these delightful finches, you'll want to understand the genetics behind these colors, and the various color mutations now being bred in captivity.

Genetics is a complicated science, but a very important one for serious aviculturists. Indiscriminate breeding can produce birds that are weak and fail to thrive, and can even pass on lethal genes that kill chicks in the eggs. To begin, let's discuss some general terms and concepts.

The Genetic Code

Every living organism is born with a carefully coded set of instructions wrapped up in its DNA. These instructions are inherited from both parents, and tell the body's cells what form to take. For each characteristic, we inherit one set of genes from our father, and one set from our mother. Our genes determine if we are tall or short, male or female, dark-haired or blond, and

A red-headed/yellow mutation.

so on. The same is true for your Gouldians. Sex and feather coloring are inherited traits.

Traits

If one genetic trait takes precedence over others, it is called a *dominant* trait. For example, if red feathers are dominant over black feathers, then all the offspring of a pure red male and a black female will have red feathers like their father, because they inherited a red dominant gene from the father. However, the offspring have also inherited a black gene from their mother. Because it is a *recessive* trait, the chicks will show no sign of black feathering, but it's in their genetic makeup. If those chicks grow up and mate with another finch that has a similar genetic makeup, then most of the chicks will be red because they inherited the dominant red gene. Some, however, might inherit a copy of their father's recessive black

TIP

Keeping Records

If you're serious about breeding Gouldians, always band your chicks and keep careful records! Without genetic records, you'll probably have little luck in selling your chicks to other aviculturists.

gene instead. In this case, if they receive a recessive gene from both parents, then they will display black feathers.

Homozygous Versus Heterozygous

It's not too difficult to understand and predict coloring when you're dealing with birds that are a "pure" color, which means they have inherited the same type of gene from both parents. This type of inheritance is called *homozygous*. It becomes a little more complicated when, as in the example, the birds display one color but are carrying a gene for a different color. These are known as "split" birds, because they possess two different genotypes--one that they display visually, and one that is hidden, or latent. This is known as *heterozygous* inheritance. The chicks described would be visually red, split to black. Breeders usually write this in a form of shorthand, and would just refer to the birds as red/black.

When you're dealing with split birds, you will have no way of judging visually what genes they carry, and what they'll pass on to their offspring. If you want to breed Gouldians with an established lineage, you will have to obtain the finches from a breeder who is keeping accurate and honest records. It's possible to determine the likely genetic makeup of the adults by tracking the color of chicks they produce in several clutches, but working backward is not always accurate, and certainly isn't any way to build a bloodline.

Sex-linked Traits

When a genetic trait can be passed down from either parent, it is called an *autosomal* genotype. Some genetic traits, however, are *sex-linked*, which means the trait is expressed on a portion of the sex chromosome. To understand what this means, you'll need to understand a little about how genes are passed. When an egg is fertilized, it combines chromosomes from the mother (ovum) and father (sperm). Both sets of chromosomes provide genetic instructions for the developing embryo, which are passed on as per our earlier discussion, with one exception. The chromosomes that control sex-linked traits are shorter in the hen, and therefore contribute only one gene for each trait that resides on that portion of the chromosome.

In Gouldians, red-masked and black-masked are sex-linked traits, which means that recessive traits passed on by the father can be expressed just as easily as dominant traits if the hen does not provide a complementary dominant gene on the female chromosome. To put it simply, male offspring will always show the dominant color, no matter which parent they receive the trait from. Female offspring receive a shorter chromosome, so they need only receive one recessive gene from their father to display the recessive color.

If you're not already confused, Gouldian genetics have another curious twist. The yellow-masked gene, which suppresses the carotenoid synthesis that normally produces red coloring, is an autosomal trait that can be passed by either parent. However, the lack of red pigment that produces the yellow or orange mask can only be seen if the bird was a red-masked finch to begin with! Because of the manner in which these traits interrelate, it means that a visually yellow-masked hen will always be homozygous, and cannot be split to any other color. A yellow-masked male can be pure yellow, or can be split to black.

If the yellow-mask trait is expressed in a visually black-masked bird, that bird will have a yellow-tipped beak. However, a black-masked bird can *carry* the yellow trait without expressing it, and in this case the beak would have a normal red tip.

Mutations

In addition to the normal color phases described above, Gouldians are now being bred in a variety of mutated colors, which we mentioned briefly in the first chapter. Mutations are "accidents" of nature that occur when normal color synthesis is changed or suppressed.

White-breasted: In the case of the white-breasted mutation, the ability to produce color in the chest feathers is lost, and resulting birds have white in place of purple feathers. White-breasted is a simple recessive trait.

Lutino: Another common mutation is the yellow or lutino color. In these birds, the gene that produces melanin is suppressed, and the only colors that can be displayed are yellow, white, and red. A lutino Gouldian will appear mostly yellow with a red or orange mask. Lutino is a sex-linked recessive trait.

Albino: Albino is a genetic mutation that suppresses all pigmentation, so these birds are pure white with red eyes, because they can't produce color even in the irises of the eye. White-colored Gouldians with dark eyes are not true albinos, because they can produce at least eye pigment.

Lethal Genes

Although many of these mutations are beautiful, they can be troublesome. Albinos, for example, tend to be weak birds that don't survive for long. As mentioned at the beginning of this chapter, in some avian species breeding for mutations has introduced a "lethal gene." This is an inherited genetic flaw that kills the embryos in the egg. I'm not aware of lethal gene combinations in Gouldians just yet, but the point is that aviculturists have a solemn responsibility to promote the welfare of the species they choose to breed. We are the stewards of this very endangered genetic material, and we must not take that responsibility lightly.

Red-headed/white-breasted mutation.

Left: Once you understand Gouldian genetics, you'll be able to closely predict the coloration of chicks before they even hatch!

Displayed Color and Genetic Composition

Male X Female	Male Offspring	Female Offspring
Visual Red-Masked Male		
RR X RR	50% RR	50% RR
Rb X RR	25% RR, 25% Rb	25% RR, 25% bb
Ry X RR	25% RR, 25% Ry	25% RR, 25% Ry
Rby X RR	12.5% RR, 12.5% Rb, 12.5% Ry, 12.5% Rby	12.5% RR, 12.5% bb, 12.5% Ry, 12.5% by
RR X Ry	25% RR, 25% Ry	25% RR, 25% Ry
Rb X Ry	12.5% RR, 12.5% Rb, 12.5% Ry, 12.5% Rby	12.5% RR, 12.5% bb, 12.5% Ry, 12.5% by
Ry X Ry	12.5% RR, 25% Ry, 12.5% yy	12.5% RR, 25% Ry, 12.5% yy
RR X bb	50% Rb	50% RR
Rb X bb	25% Rb, 25% bb	25% RR, 25% bb
Ry X bb	25% Rb, 25% Rby	25% RR, 25% Ry
Rby X bb	12.5% Rb, 12.5% by, 12.5% Rby, 12.5% bb	12.5% RR, 12.5% Ry, 12.5% bb, 12.5% by
RR X by	25% Rb, 25% Rby	25% RR, 25% Ry
Rb X by	12.5% Rb, 12.5% by, 12.5% Rby, 12.5% bb	12.5% RR, 12.5% Ry, 12.5% bb, 12.5% by
Ry X by	12.5% Rb, 25% Rby, 12.5% by	12.5% RR, 25% Ry, 12.5% yy
Rby X by	6.25% Rb, 6.25% bb, 12.5% Rby, 12.5% by, 6.25% yb, 6.25% bby	6.25% RR, 6.25% bb, 12.5% Ry, 12.5% by, 6.25% yy, 6.25% bby
RR X bby	50% Rby	50% Ry
Rb X bby	25% Rby, 25% by	25% Ry, 25% by
Ry X bby	25% Rby, 25% yb	25% Ry, 25% yy
Rby X bby	12.5% Rby, 12.5% bby, 12.5% by, 12.5% yb	12.5% Ry, 12.5% by, 12.5% yy, 12.5 % bby
RR X yy	50% Ry	50% Ry
Rb X yy	25% Ry, 25% Rby	25% Ry, 25% by
Ry X yy	25% Ry, 25% yy	25% Ry, 25% yy
Rby X yy	12.5% Ry, 12.5% Rby, 12.5% yy, 12.5% yb	12.5% Ry, 12.5% by, 12.5% yy, 12.5% bby
Rby X Ry	6.25% RR, 6.25% Rb, 12.5% Ry, 12.5% Rby, 6.25% yy, 6.25% yb	6.25% RR, 6.25% bb, 12.5% Ry, 12.5% by, 6.25% yy, 6.25% bby
Visual Black-Masked Male		
bb X bb	50% bb	50% bb
by X bb	25% bb, 25% by	25% bb, 25% by
bby X bb	50% by	50% by
bb X by	25% bb, 25% by	25% bb, 25% by

Displayed Color and Genetic Composition (continued)

Male X Female	Male Offspring	Female Offspring
Visual Black-Masked Male (continued)		
by X by	12.5% bb, 25% by, 12.5% bby	12.5% bb, 25% by, 12.5% bby
bby X by	25% by, 25% bby	25% by, 25% bby
bb X bby	50% by	50% by
by X bby	25% by, 25% bby	25% by, 25% bby
bby X bby	50% bby	50% bby
bb X RR	50% Rb	50% bb
by X RR	25% Rb, 25% Rby	25% Rb, 25% Rby
bby X RR	50% Rby	50% by
bb X Ry	25% Rb, 25% Rby	25% Rb, 25% Rby
by X Ry	12.5% Rb, 25% Rby, 12.5% yb	12.5% bb, 25% by, 12.5% bby
bby X Ry	25% Rby, 25% yb	25% by, 25% bby
bb X yy	50% Rby	50% by
by X yy	25% Rby, 25% yb	25% by, 25% bby
bby X yy	50% yb	50% bby
Visual Yellow-Masked Male		
yy X yy	50% yy	50% yy
yb X yy	25% yy, 25% yb	25% yy, 25% bby
yy X RR	50% Ry	50% Ry
yb X bb	25% Ry, 25% Rby	25% Ry, 25% by
yy X Ry	25% Ry, 25% yy	25% Ry, 25% yy
yb X Ry	12.5% Ry, 12.5% Rby, 12.5% yy, 12.5% yb	12.5% Ry, 12.5% by, 12.5% yy, 12..5% bby
yy X bb	50% Rby	50% Ry
yb X bb	25% Rby, 25% by	25% Ry, 25% by
yy X by	25% Rby, 25% yb	25% Ry, 25% yy
yb X by	12.5% Rby, 12.5% by, 12.5% yb, 12.5% bby	12.5% Ry, 12.5% by, 12.5% yy, 12.5% bby
yy X bby	50% yb	50% yy
yb X bby	25% yb, 25% bby	25% yy, 25% bby

The above chart is grouped by the displayed mask color of the male of the pair. Pairings are expressed as male genes X female genes. The *first letter* of each bird represented indicates its visual mask color. For example, Ry indicates a red-masked Gouldian split to yellow, bb indicates a pure black-masked Gouldian, yb indicates a yellow-masked Gouldian split to black, and Rby indicates a red-masked Gouldian split to both black and yellow.

R = Red mask (dominant sex-linked trait); b = Black mask (recessive sex-linked)
y = Yellow mask (recessive autosomal); bby = Black mask + yellow-tipped beak

INFORMATION

Periodicals

Bird Talk/Birds USA
P.O. Box 6050
Mission Viejo, CA 92690
(949) 855-8822
www.animalnetwork.com

Bird Times
7-L Dundas Circle
Greensboro, NC 27407
(336) 292-4047
www.birdtimes.com

The AFA Watchbird
2208 "A" Artesia Boulevard
Redondo Beach, CA 90278

Organizations

Association of Avian Veterinarians
P.O. Box 811720
Boca Raton, FL 33481
(561) 393-8901
www.aav.org

American Federation of Aviculture
P.O. Box 7312
North Kansas City, MO 64116
(816) 421-2473
www.AFAbirds.org

The National Finch and Softbill Society
www.nfss.org

The Finch Society of Australia
www.finchsociety.org

Helpful Web Sites

Finchworld
www.finchworld.com

eFinch
www.efinch.com

Lady Gouldian Finch
www.ladygouldianfinch.com

Manufacturers and Suppliers

Stromberg's
P.O. Box 400
Pine River, MN 56474
(218) 587-2222
www.info@strombergschickens.com
(aviary supplies)

Corner's Limited
841 Gibson
Kalamazoo, MI 49001
(800) 456-6780
www.cornerslimited.com
(cages)

Brinsea Products
3670 South Hopkins Avenue
Titusville, FL 32780
(407) 267-7009
(incubators, brooders, egg candlers)

Pretty Bird International, Inc.
5810 Stacy Trail
P.O. Box 177
Stacy, MN 55079
(800) 356-5020
www.prettybird.com
(seed and formulated diets)

Kaytee Products, Inc.
521 Clay Street
Chilton, WI 53014
(800) 669-9580
www.kaytee.com
(seed and treats)

L&M Bird Leg Bands
P.O. Box 2943
San Bernardino, CA 92406
(909) 882-4649
(bird leg bands)

L'Avian Pet Products
Highway 75 S
P.O. Box 359
Stephen, MN 56757
(800) 543-3308
(L'Choice bird diets)

Prevue Pet Products, Inc.
224 North Maplewood Avenue
Chicago, IL 60612
(800) 243-3624
(pet and breeding cages)

Rolf C. Hagen U.S.A. Corp.
50 Hampden Road
Mansfield, MA 02048
(800) 225-2700
www.pubnix.net/~mhagen
(various bird products, seed diets)

Valentine Inc.
4259 South Western Boulevard
Chicago, IL 60609
(800) 438-7883
(galvanized wire, cage building supplies)

Finches are attractive and relatively quiet companions.

Suggested Reading

Burgmann, Petra. *Feeding Your Pet Bird.* Hauppauge, NY: Barron's Educational Series, Inc., 1993.
Romagnano, April, and Christa Koeppf. *The Finch Handbook.* Hauppauge, NY: Barron's Educational Series, Inc., 2001.

About the Author

Gayle Soucek has been keeping and breeding a variety of exotic birds for over twenty years. She is the author of five books and numerous magazine articles on avian husbandry, nutrition, breeding, and disease. Gayle is past-President of the Midwest Avian Research Expo, the Midwest Congress of Bird Clubs, and the Northern Illinois Parrot Society. She resides near Chicago with her husband, birds, and dog.

Photo Credits

Andy Cohen: 81 (bottom); Edward Czarnetzky: 76 (bottom); Terry Dunham: 24, 81 (top), and 88 (all); Isabelle Francais: 21 (top and bottom), 25 (top), 32 (top and bottom), 36, 37 (bottom), 48 (top and bottom), 49 (bottom right), 61, 64 (top and bottom), 72, 73, 80 (top right and bottom), and 93; D. J. Feathers Aviary: 33, 37 (top), 49 (top left), and 76 (top); Paul Kwast: 80 (top left); Shutterstock: 5, 17, 28, 29, 44, 45, 53, 57, 60, and 65; and Everett Webb: 2-3, 4, 8, 9, 12 (all), 13, 16, 20, 25 (bottom), 40, 41, 49 (top right and bottom left), 52, 56, 68, 69, 77 (top and bottom), 84, 85, and 89.

Cover Photos

All cover photos by Shutterstock.

Important Note

Please remember that Gouldians are intelligent and endangered birds. Although they do not require an inordinate amount of care, they are not low maintenance pets, and should never be purchased on a whim. Please familiarize yourself with their needs in order to provide a healthy and safe environment for them, and to insure that you and your family members are able to enjoy the birds for years to come.

All inquiries should be addressed to:
Barron's Educational Series, Inc.
250 Wireless Boulevard
Hauppauge, NY 11788
www.barronseduc.com

ISBN-13: 978-0-7641-3850-8
ISBN-10: 0-7641-3850-2

Library of Congress Catalog Card No. 2007042363

Library of Congress Cataloging-in-Publication Data
Soucek, Gayle.
   Gouldian finches : everything about purchase, housing, nutrition, health care, and breeding / Gayle Soucek : illustrations by Michele Earle-Bridges.
      p. cm.
   Includes index.
      ISBN-13: 978-0-7641-3850-8 (alk. paper)
      ISBN-10: 0-7641-3850-2 (alk. paper)
      1. Gouldian finch. I. Title.

SF473.G68S68   2008
636.6'862—dc22   2007042363

Printed in China
9 8 7 6 5 4 3 2 1